Spread and Influence of Hinduism and Buddhism in Asia

Spread and Influence of Hinduism and Buddhism in Asia

Edited by

Sengaku Mayeda & Masahiro Shimoda

Originals

(an imprint of Low Price Publications)

Delhi-110052

ISBN 13: 978-81-8454-098-7

Published by
Originals
(an imprint of Low Price Publications)
A-6, Nimri Commercial Centre,
Near Ashok Vihar Phase-IV,
Delhi-110052
Phone: 27302453
e-mail: info@Lppindia.com
website: www.Lppindia.com

Printed at
D K Fine Art Press P Ltd.
Delhi-110052

PRINTED IN INDIA

Contents

Foreword

Vedic Dharma (later known as Hinduism) and Buddhism have been prominent among the oldest cultural manifestations of human intuitive, reflective and creative consciousness. Though originated in Indian sub-continent they spread and influenced all over Asia in ancient times through sea and land routes. Though earliest records of this phenomenon are not available whatever scanty information we have at present is sufficient to evince that its influence has been deep, pervasive and beneficent. There is still scope for further researches in the fields of archeology, ancient literary and philosophical writings, art forms, folk tales and lore of elderly people to go to the roots. Regarding South–East Asia Professor R.C. Majumdar in a small book, "Indian Culture in South-East Asia" remarked, "It is unfortunate that the Government, the universities and the people of free India take hardly any interest in what may justly be described as one of the most glorious episodes in the history of Indian culture, abundant traces of which still remain in remote widely scattered regions all over South Asia." (Preface, page v) Whatever he has opined about South-East Asia holds good about whole of Asia. In this regard the present work is an important contribution. The initiative taken by the Committee for Japan-India Academic Exchange to organize a symposium on the theme "Spread and Influence of Hinduism and Buddhism in Asia" and to bring out its proceedings are welcome steps. Credit for this goes to Professor Chie Nakane and Professor Sengaku Mayeda. It is hoped that the Indian side will also take a similar initiative.

The mutual relations between India and Japan have been age-old and time-honoured. In recent times they have developed very significantly along with exchanges in the fields of science and technology. Exchanges in material goods are no doubt important but they are ephemeral whereas cultural exchanges are lasting and deep. Japanese scholars have done appreciable job in renewing cultural contacts. The role of Japan Foundation and the Embassy of Japan in India needs a special mention.

In 21st century a new conception of Asia is emerging and in this respect India and Japan have to play a crucial role. Need is to transcend "western peoples' orientalist perspective of Asia". In this direction Professor Noburu Karashima's edited book entitled "Introducing India" is significant. The contributions of Late Professor Hajime Nakamura are highly important. In India Professor Lokesh Chandra and Professor K. Sankaranarayana have done useful work and they are still active. I wish both sides take greater interest for mutual enrichment and universal well being.

20.01.2010

Siddheshwar R Bhatt
MP-23, Pitam Pura,
Delhi-110034
srb39@gmail.com

Introduction

The Indian history of thought and religions opens up with those of the Ṛgveda which is said to have been compiled between 1500 BCE and 1000 BCE; the so-called Brahmanism flourished until the 5th century BCE and at that time a huge amount of Vedic literature was compiled. In the 5th century BCE Mahāvīra and Gautama Buddha founded Jainism and Buddhism respectively. Thereafter, Buddhism expanded its sphere of influence to South and North beyond the border of India at the time of Emperor Aśoka and was migrated into China in the 1st century CE via the Silk Road and further into Japan officially through Korea in the year 538 (or, 552).

Thus the official introduction of Buddhism into Japan took place in the 6th century CE, about 1000 years after the birth of Buddhism in India. In the 6th century CE, the Gupta Dynasty (320-540), which is said to be the golden age of classical culture of India, was coming to an end shortly and the so-called 6 systems of Indian philosophy, Buddhism and Jainism had established their own philosophical systems in India,

In the 6th century CE, Japanese people believed in so many gods called *kami*, respecting awe-inspiring objects as gods or *kami*, for example, the special kind of natural objects such as water, sun, wind, moon, thunder, rocks and huge trees as well such special kind of animals as serpents and foxes. They regarded those objects and animals as gods or as gods' messengers. In the term of comparative religion, philosophy and theology, such type of beliefs, which are similar to those which are seen in the Ṛgveda, is sometimes called animism or pantheism. They had no definite theoretical systems and their belief had no definite denomination at the time of official introduction of Buddhism. It was named "Shinto" or "way of gods or *kamis*" i.e. "Shintoism," only after Japanese people began to compare their beliefs with Buddhism, a foreign religion.

Before the introduction of Buddhism, in the 5th century Confucianism was migrated into Japan in such religious situations. However, it could not penetrate into Japanese mind for it was primarily a normative thought with which how to govern the state. On the other hand, Taoism was also introduced into Japan along with Buddhism in the 6th century but wane before long for it did not come with its scriptures, teachers and temples.

In such religious situation of Japan, Buddhism was transmitted along with Buddhist sutras, Buddha images, temples, highly advanced thought and culture. In the beginning the Buddha was regarded as foreign god and Buddhism was accepted as a kind of magic. Although Buddhism started as a kind of magic, it was gradually more and more deeply and systematically understood and developed into Japanese Buddhism. It was Prince Shotoku (574-622) who laid the foundation for the prosperity of Buddhism in Japan which finally came to form an influential Japanese religion and thought.

It is indeed true that the influence of Buddhism over Japanese culture, literature, thought, religion, mental attitudes, daily life, customs and the like has been so deep and wide that we can hardly talk about things Japanese without referring to Buddhism. However, most Japanese seem to feel themselves indebted far more to China than to Korea or India for Buddhism.

The Buddhism which was first introduced into Japan from Korea was of course Korean Buddhism. But in 607 Prince Shotoku sent Ono Imoko as envoy to the Sui Dynasty of China along with

Buddhist monks. Since then Chinese Buddhism and culture, which had so far been introduced into Japan via Korea, came to be imported directly from China with many Japanese monks who went to China to study Buddhism there. As a result the importance of Korea as the source of Buddhism and culture came to be gradually lost and forgotten. All the Buddhist texts read and used in Japan were what were translated into and/or written in Chinese and/or in Japanese. Even Buddhist monk Bodhisena, probably the first Indian who came to Japan, did not arrive directly from India but from China in 736 CE where he stayed for some time. India was regarded as an extremely remote country and Japan was called "Hendo" (= Remote country) by Japanese people in those days. There was no opportunity for the Japanese to study Indian Buddhism until the year 1884 when Bun'yu Nanjo (1819-1892) returned to Japan after having studied Sanskrit and Indian Buddhism for eight years under F. Max Müller (1823-1900) at Oxford University.

From October, 1998 to March, 1999 I was given an opportunity to deliver a series of lectures entitled, "An Invitation to Indian Philosophy with Special Reference to Veda and Upaniṣads" once a week for general listeners through the NHK radio and prepared a text book for this purpose. The first two chapters entitled "Japan and India" and "India in Japan" were dedicated to an explanation as to how wide and deep are Indian influences over Japanese language, culture, and religion by showing many concrete examples, although the Indian influences are not apparent to the present average Japanese people as the Chinese influences.

For the purpose of making my explanation more persuasive and appealing to the listeners who have no knowledge of India and Indian philosophy, I quoted a subject "Indian Influence" (pp. 306-308) from a encyclopaedic work entitled *Things Japanese*, Being Notes on Various Subjects Connected with Japan composed by a famous British Japanologist B.H. Chamberlain (1850-1935) (Rutland, Vennont & Tokyo: Charles E. Turtle Co., 15th printing, 1984); he came to Japan at the age of 23 in 1873 and stayed here in Japan for about 40 years.

On the subject "Indian Influence" Chamberlain says as follows:

In a sense Japan may be said to owe everything to India; for from India came Buddhism, and Buddhism brought civilization, Chinese civilization; but then China had been far more deeply tinged with the Indian dye than is generally admitted even by the Chinese themselves. The Japanese, while knowing, of course? full well that Buddhism is Indian, not only habitually underrate the influence of Buddhism in great matters; they have no adequate notion of the way in which smaller details of their lives and thoughts have been molded by it. (p. 246)

Then Chamberlain shows many examples such as several Japanese customs, the arranging of the Japanese syllabaries, some of current fairy-tales, and Japanese words derived from Sanskrit which are used even in the Japanese daily life.

His remarks, "In a sense Japan may be said to owe everything to India" can not be true any longer in modern Japan which has been increasingly westernized and industrialized year by year, but might have been true to a considerable extent in his days, i.e. in early 1900s when he wrote the book. Today such deep and wide Indian influence over Japan is not felt by the average Japanese people.

As for Hinduism, it has never been officially introduced into Japan. In India Buddhism is regarded as a sect of Hinduism or a hinduism for export while in Japan Hinduism is generally regarded as a foreign religion totally different from Buddhism. However, as you know, Hinduism was originally in a parent-child relationship with Buddhism, and a lot of Hindu elements were absorbed into Buddhism. Hinduism is so inseparably and secretly fused with Buddhism that it is hardly possible for the average Japanese to distinguish Hindu elements from Buddhism.

For example, the teachings of *karman* and *saṃsāra*, which originated from Upaniṣads and are in essence heterogeneous with Buddhist standpoint of *anātmavāda*, i.e. "non-soul theory," play a very important role in Buddhism, Indian and Chinese as well as Japanese. Nevertheless, in Japan the concepts of *karman* and *saṃsāra* have generally been regarded as a special feature of Buddhism without knowing their origins in Hinduism (or, Brahmanism).

Many Hindu gods such as Indra, Sarasvatī and Gaṇeśa have been worshipped by Japanese people without any consciousness that they are of Hindu origin. It is really a wonder that two Hindu philosophical texts, i.e. the Chinese versions of *Suvarṇasaptati* (tr. into Chinese by Paramārtha) and *Daśapadārthaśāstra* (tr. into Chinese by Hsuan-tsang), crept into the Chinese Buddhist Canon. Hinduism is, so to speak, a *pracchannabauddhadarśana*, namely "Buddhism in disguise." In this sense the influence of Hinduism over Japan has been indirect and implicit but never negligible.

Then a thought occurred to me: The Japanese, consciously or unconsciously, have or had been to some extent in common with the Indian in their thought, culture, religion and the like through Buddhism. Nevertheless, the Japanese today look westwards which is more or less heterogeneous with themselves and they are rather indifferent to India and Hinduism, the roots of their religion, thought, and culture. K. V. Kesavan, Professor of Jawaharlal Nehru University, rightly comments of this situation: "Despite age-old cultural bonds, common political sysems and institutions, and complementary economies, the two countries have developed cool and calculating attitudes towards each other (*Towards Understanding Each Other: Fifty Years' History of India-Japan Mutual Studies*, ed. by Chie Nakane and Masao Naito, Tokyo: Committee for Japan-India Academic Exchange, 1999, p. 17).

Why are the two countries in such an undesirable and unfortunate situation? Why don't they look directly at each other? Japan should make more efforts to understand India through Hinduism which might be a parent of Buddhism, and India should pay more attention to Japan through Japanese Buddhism, which might be a grandson of Hinduism. In this context a joint Indo-Japanese seminar was held by the Committee for Japan-India Academic Exchange at Tokyo International Forum, Tokyo, on 10-11 June 2000 under the auspices of the Japan Society for the Promotion of Science (JSPS) and the Indian Council of Social Science Research (ICSSR) and in generous collaboration of Indian Embassy in Tokyo. A large number of distinguished scholars, graduate students, and journalists participated in the seminar. On this occasion 10 papers were presented by scholars from both India and Japan. Among them 7 papers have been included in this volume and they deal with different topics of Hinduism and Buddhism in Asia including Japan.

The late Professor R.R. Pandey takes up one of the key concepts of Indian philosophy, *karma* and its relation in the conception of *saṃsāra* for his main discussion in the paper suitably entitled as "Concept of *Karma* and *Saṃsāra* in Indian and Japanese Culture." Here, he argues against the general misconception of this important concept by the modern thinkers that this conception warrants humans to accept 'indolence and inertia' or implicit acceptance of what is termed as 'fate.' To this clichéd argument, Pandey opines that if properly conceived, *karma* denotes freewill and individual choices, because one has to own up responsibility for all his actions in his worldly life. He gives an excellent hermeneutical interpretation of *karma* from Vedic period to the contemporary times. Notably in the essay, Pandey tries to understand the theory of *karma* from the Upaniṣadic discussions. He explains various facets of karma such as *saṃcita karma, prārabdha karma and āgami karma*, and argue that how individual choices and freewill is protected in karma theory. In this worldly existence, humans only have the liberty to perform karma effectively and therefore human life is valued highly even to the worldly existence of the gods. The *saṃsāra* can be explained as the realm of human life in the world which is imperfect, so the individual personality can find perfection by performing karma in this world (*saṃsāra*) Human beings born again and again in this world therefore *saṃsāra* is rebirth too. Panday then equates the influence of desire (*vāsanā*) with the worldly existence and explains how rebirth can remove desire (*vāsanā*). The individual personality attains perfection from imperfection. In the Western (Christian) religious tradition, divine grace is what determines the existence of the individual person in the worldly life, and in the modern scientific approach individual life is determined by materialistic rationalism. Pandey considers the conception of *karma* and *saṃsāra* in relation to these western ideas.

By explaining the conception of *karma* and *saṃsāra* in Buddhism he tries to explain its importance in Asian culture. Especially, in the Japanese culture, the idea of *karma* is conceived as a person's dedication to his duty and his commitment to fulfill it. Pandey concludes that this is the secret of the success of industrial development in Japan in recent times.

Professor S. R. Bhatt deals with Buddha as a body of ideas as the main theme of discussion in his paper entitled "The Concepts of Buddha and Bodhisattva."

He gives an excellent exposition of the '*Karuṇā* centrality' of Buddhism and explains the importance of universal compassion (*mahākaruṇā*), adequate endeavour (*upāya kauśala*) for achieving excellence in one's life. He posits that *mahākaruṇā* is the motivating force for Buddhist spiritual self culture, i.e. *prajñā*, *śīla* and *samādhi*. Notably, Bhatt tries to explain the philosophical meaning of many Buddhistic terms so as to give a comprehensive and rational understanding of Buddhism. For example he explains the conception of *prajñā* and its relation with *karuṇā* as the main spiritual realization (*bodhicitta*) of an aspirant (*Bodhisattva*). He equates *karuṇā* with the deep love of the Buddha, which transcends all barriers and reaches to anyone who is in suffering as the nature of *karuṇā* that is to be inculcated by any aspirant for realizing *bodhicitta*. He argues also that the conception of *Dharmakāya*, in fact, is the all pervasive oneness of the humanity and that oneness can be realized by realizing *bodhicitta*. He goes on to say that the Buddha and Bodhisattvas are, in other words, *karuṇā* reincarnated. Therefore emancipation of everyone (*sarvamukti*) is the goal of the Buddha and the Bodhisattva.

The practice of *brahmavihāras* and *pāramitās* of a Bodhisattva is *karuṇā*-centric; so also the conception of *śūnyatā*, and the realization of *niḥsvabhāvatā* is rooted in *karuṇā*. In the conception of *nirvāṇa*, the intellectual aspect, *prajñā* and the emotional aspect, *karuṇā* are important as propounds the annihilation of ego, desires and false identification with objects of the world.

With the interpretation of *Dharmakāya* he explains the deep concern of Buddhist philosophy towards ecology and sustenance of the ecosystem which is an expression of *Mahākaruṇā*. He is also of the opinion that the Buddhist philosophy is beyond the confines of the materialistic perspective of life. Bhatt, in this paper, quotes extensively from Buddhist and Brahmanical sources to highlight the importance of *karuṇā* in the discourses of Indian philosophy.

Professor Musashi Tachikawa treats the concept of transmigration in his paper entitled: "The *Jātaka* and Self-sacrifice."

Though the idea of the transmigration of the soul was rejected by Śākyamuni Buddha, the later Buddhists due to the influence of Hinduism more or less accepted this idea. Most of these Buddhists are of the idea that transmigration happens due to the *karmic* influence which is in contrast to the views of the Brahmins who believe that the permanent soul of a being transmigrates from one birth to another.

This difference may be due to the idea that the physical body is influenced by *karma* more than the soul. On this topic, Thachikawa makes a comparative exposition of the Hindu and the Buddhist views. He also explains: Disregarding the doctrinal differences, some Buddhists believe in the transmigration of the soul as the Hindus. He argues that when the power of *karma* leaves the body, one enters into *Nirvāṇa*. A true follower of Buddhism may not choose to be born again in this world, because teachings underlie the fact that the life in the world is full of sufferings, whereas the Hindus consider the human body as an entity that survives only for a life span extending only for a few years of life in this world, but the soul is eternal.

Tachikawa is of the opinion that the general believers of the Buddhism today prefer rebirth. This problem is common in all religions. The *Jātaka* stories may not agree with the teachings of Śākyamuni Buddha, because he denied the existence of any previous lives possible for anybody. But in the religious history of Buddhism we can see various kinds of representations and motifs in places like Bhārhut, Sañchī, Amarāvatī and the like from the stories of Śākyamuni's previous lives. Based on the original teaching *Jātakas* should not be considered as a Buddhist scripture.

The stories of *Jātaka* are all denoting the *Parinir vāṇa* of the Śākyamuni and teach us that the final *nirvāṇa* can be achieved, if one decides to renounce his worldly life. And most of the stories have the moral of following good *karma* for acquiring merit to enter into *nirvāṇa.* The morals of these stories that suggest good *karma* as a way of life are more relevant today than ever before. There may be inconsistencies between the original teaching of the historical personality of Śākyamuni Buddha that rejects transmigration of soul and stories in the *Jātaka*, but they give a supreme teaching on the virtue of good *karma* and self sacrifices.

Professor Masahiro Shimoda aims at stressing the importance of introducing new histroiographical method in constructing the history of the Buddha in his article entitled "The Revival of the Buddha in Narratives: "The Conflict between Philology and the Science of History."

He highlights the problem of a scholar to account the historical Buddha and the mythological Buddha. Most of the Japanese scholars of Buddhist history uses the scientifically inconsistent method introduced by Hajime Nakamura which is restricting them to select the research materials that is required for scientifically consistent historical works. He argues that the work of Nakamura entitled *Gautama Buddha* is simply like a presentation of sorted data ('notcard style).

Most of the Buddhist historians have taken on the method of Nakamura without proper introspection on to those inconsistencies; at least they should have noticed the difference between historical science and philology. Each of the studies on philology and on historical science has its own purposes to fulfill. But if we would not distinguish them properly, we might make a mistake. Now we have many available histriographical tools which could reveal the ' historical Buddha' in better light.

In this respect we can see that the historical studies are at the primary stage. Historical studies on Buddha in the west tried to explain the history of Buddha based on preconceived ideas and speculations, using a very little material. Some scholars tried establish 'the origin of Buddha in Ethiopia.' Most of those inconsistent studies on the 'history of Buddha' appeared in 19th century eventually become the primary sources for further academic research. Western scholars were trapped in the controversy between the mythical stories connected with the Buddha and the verifiable historical facts. Shimoda refers to the suggestion by Emile Senart on this, and reasons out clearly that the methodological constraints in the historical studies of the Buddha hampered its smooth progress. Shimoda suggests that, instead of creating a methodological limbo, the scholars need to restructure the historical aspects of Buddha and see the mythological aspects from the historical perspective. In fact the Buddhist canon provides ample material for such an approach. Shimoda also points out the attempt of some western scholars to construct the concept of the Buddha as similar to that of the Christ (Messiah), the saviour of the world. The Buddhist studies in fact in 19th and 20th century fell into the realm of Eurocentric concerns and world views where protestant Christian ideologies had taken the prime position.

Shimoda asserts that, when we collect the sources for constructing a history of the Buddha, we need to segregate the material on the basis of 'what he said' and 'what is said about him;' in this case a scholar confronts a lot of interpretational issues. In certain cases the texts are exclusively read to interpret the historicity of the Buddha as in the case of many leading scholars who read the text in this way, leaving no room for criticism. In the contemporary text based historical studies we can see the method of treating a text based on two aspects : "documentary aspect" and "work-like aspect." These methods could lead the reader who lives in the present to be taken to the time of the writing of the text. A kind of hermeneutic experience is imparted to the reader where a huge space for understanding is invoked. This method would provide ample space of self-reflection to the Buddhist follower rather than just hearing stories or myths.

In the present context Shimoda's idea of redefining the history of Buddha is worth noticing. Buddhism is a world religion now; it has grown beyond India and Asia. Today the Buddha belong to the world not just to India or Asia, therefore the religio-philosophical view of Buddhism is juxtaposed with all other systems of thought from around the world; contextually Shimoda interprets it as: "'Being historical' means, among other things, the state of being transformed and generated"

Professor Shinji Shigematsu focuses on a very important ritualistic festival of the Tamil immigrant community in Malaysia in his paper "The Ritual of *Tai Pūsam* and the Role of *Pandāram* in Malaysia." The festival of *Tai Pūsam* is mainly conducted by the expatriate Tamil diasporas in various parts of the world and it is getting extinct in India. In this context this paper is of extreme importance, especially to researches who study about Tamil culture. The study in this paper is based on the festival of *Tai pûsam* taken place at a plantation company and explains how this festival is conducted and explains the role of the *Pandâram*, the traditional non-Brahmin Tamil priest as chief priest of the festival.

The Tamil migrants, who went to Malay to work in the plantations, took with them several religious festivals, and among them *Tai Pūsam* is the most important one. This fervour of the festival shows the cultural identity of the Tamils that have become a part of this festival. Shigematsu gives a narrative about the legends and myths surrounding the godhead of Murugan or Subramanyan on whose name the festival is celebrated. Murugan is a highly revered godhead among the Tamil population around the world. Murugan is patent deity for several communities in the Tamil culture. Shigematsu gives the graphic details of various communities and castes that participate in the festival, duties of each in the festival, and how the financial system and funding of the festival is done.

There are many secular socio-cultural activities which happen during the period of the festival. One of the important aspects of this festival is that it is meant to initiate cultural understanding between Tamil communities and others in the plantation area; therefore the company takes an active interest in the conduct of the festival. There is a long description about the *Pandāram* priest who is not from the traditional Brahmin caste. There are several temples in Tamil Nadu where such priests are performing the rituals, especially at the temples of Amman (mother goddess), Murugan and Ayyanar. The narration on this gives a lot of knowledge about the non-Brahmin spiritual culture of the Tamil people in the world. Almost all participants of various functions of the festivities are participating as a devotee of the God Murugan where he considers all activities are sacrifices to the God. Therefore the person who participates gains personal merit (*puṇya*). The penitents, who participate in the rituals, are the main attraction of the festival. They normally take a vow that they would participate as a penitent in the festivities for acquiring merit (*puṇya*). In this case the family members of such penitents also get the same merit and virtue from the god Murugan.

As we can see in a world where spiritual life and community life are fast getting extinct, the study of Shigematsu on the Tamil community is of multiple values. The ethnography of the rituals and traditions of the Tamil people, the importance of community spiritual culture, and most significantly the value of spiritual self culture in social life, are the few points one can learn from this paper.

Dr. Sudha Malaiya mainly discusses the dancing image of Gaṇeśa as a worshipping deity and its spread within India and other parts of the world in her paper "Dancing Gaṇeśa in India and beyond its Frontiers." Here the main description is based on central India but ample references are made from other parts of the world where Gaṇeśa images are found. She also gives a picture of the spread of Indian culture and religion together with this popularization of the image of Gaṇeśa. The dancing Gaṇeśa and dancing Śiva have similarities but their expressions are different and Malaiya gives a descriptive picture of those differences. There are descriptions on various iconographical properties of the godhead dancing Gaṇeśa and its relation to iconography of dancing Śiva. She gives a descriptive analysis of the transitional process of the dancing Gaṇeśa image and its relation to various types of Gaṇeśa. In India Gaṇeśa is considered as a Hindu deity at present, but in other part of Asia Gaṇeśa is accepted as a Buddhist deity.

After establishing the iconographic properties of the dancing Gaṇeśa in central India, Malaiya explains how this image is represented in the Kotan, Mongolia, Afghanistan, and Nepal. Especially in the images of Nepal, she describes the elements of both Buddhist and Hindu gods with the images of Gaṇeśa. The Buddhist aspect of Gaṇeśa together with Hindu images can be seen in the representations in Burma, Thai, Indochina and Indonesia. This study calls for further studies on this topic in China and Japan.

Dr. Malaiya's study is a rich source of information to those who are interested in Indian iconography especially the dance sculptures, especially those who want to study on the iconography of Gaṇeśa in central India.

Professor N. Vijaya introduces the issue of protecting the environment and how this issue was addressed by the Hindu religious tradition and culture in her article entitled "Environment Perspective of Hindu Festivals."

She focuses on the festival rituals where the protection of environment is delicately imbibed into each of those rituals. The performance of those rituals shows us how great was the concern that the ancient cultures had on the environment. She starts her discussion on this issue from the religiosity of most of the ancient cultures to environment that most of them considered earth as the mother of all living beings. She also gives picture of this aspect in the Vedic rituals and how the later Hindu rituals propitiated it in various forms of other rituals. However, she describes few festivals of great importance in the religious culture of the Hindus as the main theme of her discussion.

The depiction of *Vasantotsava* (spring festival), which is now celebrated as *Holi* and the implications of various rituals and performance connected with it in an elaborate manner. In the same way, the implied meanings of the rituals connected with other various festivals are also described in an articulate way. *Ugadi*, a festival celebrated by Telugu and Kannada peoples of South India, *Saṃkrānthi* which is celebrated in almost all parts of India in different names. The festival of *Daśara* which is celebrated for nine days, the festival *Vijayadaśami*, etc. are a few of them. She explains various medicinal and environmental properties of things used in these festivals.

In today's industrialised culture human beings are hugely distanced themselves from the nature and natural things. As we can see in this article most of those rituals and materials used in those rituals are environmentally important. It is not just good for the environment of the earth but also for the smooth and healthy conduct of human life. These festivals are thousands of years old and the rituals have tested years of observation and study; therefore, what is implied in these rituals is a part of ancient wisdom. We must appreciate it with the due respect that it calls for when we think about the environmental issues today.

Prof. J. K. Bajaj's paper "Relevance of Mahatma Gandhi and His Thought in Modern Times" mainly talks about the spiritual idea of *Sanatana dharma* and how it shaped the personality of Mahatma Gandhi as a human being, and how he conceived the idea of *Swaraj* as a political ideology from its foundation. *Sanatana dharma* was also central when he explained the idea of *Satyagraha*, and most importantly how he viewed the influence of technology in human society. The whole paper gives a comprehensive idea how Indians viewed the individual life of a human personality, his inherent right over his land of birth and tradition, his right to protest if such rights are infringed by any authority whether internal or external. This is the sphere of *dharma*. The state that protects the *dharma* of all living beings is named as *Swaraj*. In this way of looking the conception of *Swaraj* and the modern idea of nation state is characteristically different. In the case of nation state, the state lay down the law based on various considerations and insists the citizens to follow the rules to be a part of it. On the other hand, the conceptions of *Swaraj* look into the inherent rights of each individual, community, society based on their inherent rights and duties (*dharma*). The main difference we can experience in the case of law enforcement, where the modern society attaches over emphasis on retribution and punishment; whereas, in the conception of *Swaraj* it should be based on compassion to the individual and deeper understanding of the situation. One of the aspects that is against the idea of *Swaraj* is the centralization of authority and power. In the present situation in the world with globalization we can see a kind of centralization of business activities and the nation state authorized centralized power structures. They are, in fact, detecting authority everywhere leaving a lot of discontented and disillusioned people who cannot find a way to express their grievances. In the Gandhian conception, *Satyagraha* (insistence on truth) is a way in which one can win back his lost freedom of such inhuman and authoritarian systems. It can be interpreted as: 'tell me the truth why my rights and duties as a human being is denied to me.' The people who take *Satygraha* as a means of protest try not to accept the dictates of the authority but never use violence to change such dictates by creating fear and haste. They want the authorities to understand the situation and take a compassionate and humane decision. They want the authorities to talk their true mind and give them the truth of everything (*satya*). The Gandhian ideals of *Ramarajya* are worth noticing here. The empire of Rama is taken as a sovereign that protects the *dharma* of all subjects. In that sense it is the *Dharmarajya.*

The most noticeable part of this paper is on the Gandhian apprehensions on the spread of technology and how men could fall into a trap of being controlled by it. Now big companies can function and produce huge profit with little human resource support. Today even in most of the so- called developed countries the number of people losing their bread winning jobs and becoming poor is a common sight. The value of human dignity is lost somewhere in our contemporary globalized society. The concept of democracy and the institutions created to support its values are under the fanciful control of a superstructure, the corporate interests and their greed to dominate the business world. It is not just the ideals of *Santana dharma* and *Swaraj* that is threatened here, but the very questions of human existence. No one is safe today, because the rationality of technology made us all function alike with the precision and efficiency of machines. Perhaps, this might have been the situation Mahatma Gandhi feared most, about the future of the world, when he spoke against uncontrolled spread of technology.

A cultural exchange agreement between Japan and India was signed in New Delhi on May 24, 1957 and the two countries agreed to observe the 50th anniversary of conclusion of the agreement, which fell in 2007, as "Japan-India Friendship Year." Therefore, about 400 commemorative events such as "lecture series" and "drama performances in Hindi and Urdu," the basic theme of which was to show "historical and cultural ties between India and Japan from the introduction of Buddhism into Japan till the modern times and their development in order to deepen the understanding between people of Japan and India regarding long historical connections between India and Japan and the fact of commonality based on this foundation. A result of the above mentioned "lecture series" was published as a book entitled *Path from India, Path from Japan: Lecture Series on Japan-India Relations*, compiled by me (New Delhi: Northern Book Centre, 2008).

Although the joint Indo-Japanese seminar was unrelated with the events of the Japan-India Friendship Year and meant mainly for the academic exchange between India and Japan, it had almost the same objective with them. It is sincerely hoped that this publication of the above 7 papers which were the products of the seminar will contribute to enhancing the mutual understanding between India and Japan.

The 5th Japan-India Seminar started with a message by Mr. C. Rajasekhar, then First Secretary, Embassy of India in Tokyo, for the Ambassador of India. Another message was delivered by Professor Chie Nakane, Member of the Japan Academy, who had long been leading and guiding the Committee of Japan-India Academic Exchange in the fields of Social Sciences and Humanities as Chairperson. Professor Noboru Karshima and the other Committee members had always been cooperative with me. Professor Haruka Yanagisawa had perfectly fulfilled his responsibility as Secretary of the Committee of Japan-India Academic Exchange. Professor Masahiro Shimoda, one of the 7 contributors, took care of all necessary detailed arrangements of the seminar in collaboration with me, the organizer of the seminar. The 7 contributors kindly took great trouble to write and to further rewrite their excellent papers due to the lapse of time and in accordance with the book style. Professor S.R. Bhatt, leader of the Indian delegates and one of the 7 contributors, was kind enough to write a Foreword and to find the publisher of this book. Dr. Mathew Varghese made great efforts to edit this book. Without their warm friendship, strong cooperation, and heartfelt assistance I could never have published this book which might be a symbol of Japan-India Friendship. My profoundest and sincerest gratitude is due to all of them. I am also very grateful to the financial assistance by the Japan Society for the Promotion of Science and the Indian Council of Social Science Research and to the friendly cooperation of the Indian Embassy in Tokyo as well as the Indian Council of Philosophical Research.

October 10, 2009

Sengaku Mayeda
President,
The Eastern Institute, Tokyo

The Concepts of Buddha and Bodhisattva

Siddheshwar R. Bhatt

In this paper I attempt to deal with the concepts of Buddha and Bodhisattva as they are understood philosophically rather than historically, even though historical perspectives cannot be divorced from the philosophical viewpoints. Śākyamuni or Gautama, the Buddha, is at the same time both a historical personality and a body of ideas. The latter, viz. Buddha as a body of ideas, is taken into consideration here: also the paper does not refer to a particular Bodhisattva as in the Buddhist tradition. The basic objective, here, is to put forth those ideas and ideals and beliefs and practices for which the concepts of Buddha and Bodhisattva stand. Though from the historical perspective, the Buddha and the Bodhisattvas have lived by these ideas and ideals, yet, in this paper, I only analyze the latter aspect for pragmatic purposes, so that they may be universalized and emulated in this world of contemporary times which is strife-torn and violence-infected. This paper specially focuses on the *karuṇā*-centricity of these concepts and on correlating them for the enhancement of the quality of life for achieving excellence. *Mahākaruṇā* or universal compassion is not just something to be thought over or talked about but to be translated in to action through proper and adequate endeavour (*upāya kauśala*). *Mahākaruṇā*, therefore, must fructify in enhancement of quality of life and achievement of excellences (*pāramitās*).

Mahākaruṇā is the starting point and the motivating force of the teachings of the Buddha in the triple facets of *prajñā*, *śīla* and *samādhi*. An attempt is made here to correlate all significant Buddhist concepts and practices with the conception of *karuṇā*.[1]

The concepts of *karuṇā* and *Mahākaruṇā* play a pivotal rôle in the Buddhist way of thinking and way of living. Beginning with the inevitable experience of *duḥkha* and an intense longing for its eradication, the entire Buddhist teaching has dovetailed to the advocacy of the pursuit for an enlightened course of conduct (*bodhicaryā*) which is motivated and guided by the altruistic feeling of *karuṇā*, an all-embracing universal love. *Karuṇā* is natural and innate to all living beings but it needs to be developed and perfected through the proper cultivation of body, will and mind.

Buddhism has not been a speculative philosophical system but a practical philosophical system (*darśana*) in which Mahākaruṇā is a distinguishing feature. The conception of the enlightenment of Śākyamuni is not of a theoretical doctrine consisting in the formulation of a well-knit thought system which is logically coherent and linguistically compact. On the other hand, it stands for the realisation of the inner and intrinsic unity and the interdependent character of all the beings, in the realm of the entire cosmos as the conception of dependent co-arising (*pratītyasamutpāda*). The doctrine of Dharmakāya also implies a globalised outlook, a *mahāprajñā* which spontaneously issues forth in *mahākaruṇā*.

All significant Buddhist concepts and practices centre on *mahāprajñā* and *mahābodhi*, and its dynamic aspect of *mahākaruṇā*. *Prajñā* and *karuṇā* are two facets of the bodhi-situation. *Prajñā* is not abstract or barren state of existence but must blossom and fructify in *karuṇā*. *Prajñā* without *karuṇā* is lame and *karuṇā* without *prajñā* is blind. I wish to mention here that though it is highlighted in Mahāyāna Buddhism[2] as one of its important teachings, and aptly taken into consideration in other cultural traditions of India *karuṇā* should be an ideal prescription for the emulation of all the cultural traditions of the world. But the centricity which it has acquired in Buddhism is something unique which makes it attractive and fascinating.

To begin with, Śākyamuni, the Buddha, is the very embodiment of *karuṇā*. He possesses a loving heart which is extended to all beings without distinction. Out of compassion for all beings languishing in suffering he preached the dharma, not to a selected group of people, but to the entire suffering masses. He was motivated by the loving mercy to help the whole universe (*sarvalokānukampā*). He loves all creatures as his own children, as says in the Saddharmapuṇḍarīka (228.4). The Buddha is distinguished from all other beings for his *mahākaruṇā*, for his intense longing and strenuous effort to alleviate the suffering of the masses. D. T. Suzuki in "Outlines of Mahāyāna Buddhism" (pp. 273-4) discusses it in detail how the Buddha works out the plan for universal redemption in all possible ways. The Buddha attained omniscience in order that he may liberate the world.

The Buddha is basically a Dharmakāya[3] which incorporates the unity or oneness of all existence, which is the source of the eternal stream of love, compassion, sympathy and mercy. This never drying stream of *karuṇā* is experienced as flowing out spontaneously from the fountainhead of Dharmakāya which is a sustaining force and also a loving heart: It is *karuṇā* and *bodhi*. All existences are one in Dharmakāya. It is considered as the organised totality of things, a principle of cosmic unity. This is not a cold and lifeless metaphysical principle, but an inexhaustible fountainhead of love and compassion. Suzuki (pp. 233-4) describes the nature, characteristics and role of Dharmakāya in detail where he quotes a Mahāyānasūtra as follows:

With one great loving heart

The thirsty desires of all beings he quencheth with coolness refreshing;

With compassion, of all doth he think

Which like space knows no bounds;

Over the world's all creation

With no thought of particularity he revieweth,

With a great heart compassionate and loving,

All sentient beings by him are embraced;

With means (upāya) which are pure, free from stains and all excellent,

He doth save and deliver all creatures innumerable,

With unfathomable love and with compassion,

All creations caressed by him universally;

Yet free from attachment his heart is.

As his compassion is great and is infinite,

Bliss unearthly on every being he confereth,

And himself showeth all over the universe;

He'll not rest till all Buddhahood truly attains.

(*Avataṃsaka-sūtra*, Chap. 13)

Like the Buddha, the Bodhisattvas are also incarnations of *karuṇā*. A Bodhisattva is characterized by *bodhicitta* and *bodhicaryā* both of which are directed towards universal welfare (*yathābhūtadarśino bodhisattvasya sattveṣu mahākaruṇā pravartate:* Bodhicaryāvatārapañjikā, 9.1). A Bodhisattva, as a *kalyāṇamitra*, exhibits his *karuṇā* mainly by taking effort to resolve the suffering and torments of others, at the same time, striving for the enlightenment of others. He consciously postpones his own emancipation till such time everyone else gets redemption. The thought of enlightenment arises in him for the welfare and liberation of all living beings (*sarvamukti*). He is an 'engaged Buddhist' actively participating in activities for social upliftment. He is happy in the happiness of others and unhappy when they are unhappy. He is a manifestation of Dharmakāya, whose motives, efforts and actions are the pivot on which the furtherance of universal welfare is possible. He is concerned with the alleviation of the suffering of others even at the cost of his own comforts. He possesses *mahākaruṇācitta* from which there is spontaneous outburst of *karuṇā* for all sentient beings without any distinction or discrimination.[4]

A Bodhisattva is comparable to one who achieved the *sthitaprajña* of the Bhagavadgītā who has *samadṛṣṭi* and who is *sarvabhūtahite rataḥ*. Both are characterized by the equanimity of mind, realization of the similarity, and commonality of experience with all the sentient beings. Benevolent temper permeates their lives in a natural way. Both are free beings but their freedom is altruistic, not self-centered. A Bodhisattva practices four psycho-physical modes of living known as, the *brahma vihāras* viz. *maitrī, karuṇā, muditā* and *upekṣā*, which are not to be viewed in discreteness or in isolation. Here also there is centricity of *karuṇā* and the remaining three are its correlates. *Maitrī* is the basis of *karuṇā*. It stands for love, respect and care for all living beings. It is the lived concreteness of loving kindness based on the feeling that just as our lives are precious to us, the lives of others are also precious. *Muditā* is the altruistic sympathetic joy. It is the happiness in the happiness of all, a consequence of *karuṇā*. *Upekṣā* is the prerequisite of *karuṇā*. It stands for compassion to all beings, which means equanimity of mind apart from impartiality.

Like the *brahma vihāras* all the *pāramitās*, six or ten, pertain to *karuṇā*. They are *dāna, śīla, kṣānti, vīrya, dhyāna, prajñā, upāya, praṇidhāna,*[6] *bala* and *jñāna*. Out of these *dāna pāramitā* is specifically related to *karuṇā*. *Dāna pāramitā* consists of charity and the renunciation of the fruits of charity. *Śīla pāramitā* is related to *karuṇā*, as it helps one in preserving *ātmabhāva* for *parārtha*. *Kṣānti pāramitā* provide bedrock to karuṇā and stands for forbearance, tolerance, patience, endurance, forgiving, non-perturbation in suffering etc. Through *vīrya pāramitā* merciful acts are performed. It helps in cultivating strength for enduring and active altruism by providing inexhaustible energy. It comprises of *upāya kauśala* in association with the four *pratisaṃvids* of *dharma, artha, nirukti* and *pratibhāna*. All the *pāramitās* help in making *karuṇā* effective.

The conception of *Śūnyatā*, which Nāgārjuna equates with *pratītyasamutpāda*, is the central teaching of Buddhism. In the empirical context it advocates *niḥsvabhāvatā* of all existence. This idea has a double-edged effect as, when viewed positively, it implies sameness of all existence, and viewed negatively it means the cultivation of *anātmabhāva* which paves the way for the experience of the sameness. The experience of *śūnyatā* of all existence develops a kind of mind-set which generates compassion (arouses *karuṇā*), which enables one to accept the suffering of others as one's own suffering, and helps to sacrifice one's own welfare for the sake of others. Through *bodhi* alone there is the possibility of the realization of *śūnyatā* of all existence. *Anātmabhāva* is the application of *śūnyatā*.

The cultivation of selflessness (or egolessness to be precise) provides a basis for the widening of the self. The doctrine of *anityatā* leads to *anātmabhāva* and this, in turn, prepares the ground for community living (*saṃgha jīvana*) and this further facilitates the social cohesion. Only through social cohesion can suffering be alleviated and be peace realized.

One of the implications of the doctrine of *pratītyasamutpāda* is interrelatedness of all existence in the ever expanding network of relationship. This is expressed as "*sarvam sarvātmakam.*" A similar idea has also been put forth in the Bhagavadgītā: "*sarvabhūtastham ātmānam sarvabhūtāni cātmani*" (6.29).

This idea of interrelatedness helps in transcending the distinction between '*sva*' and '*para*.' One who overcomes this distinction alone can work for the totality. But one who works for the totality works for oneself as well. So in selflessness there is the merger of '*sva*' and '*para*' and this solves the problem of egoism and altruism. Out of selflessness the precedence of *mahākaruṇā* occurs.

In Buddhism the attainment of *nirvāṇa* is the ultimate destiny and goal of all existents. The positively understood *nirvāṇa* is self-fulfillment through *karuṇā*. It consists in universal love for all beings. *Prajñā* is the intellectual aspect and *karuṇā*, the emotional aspect of *nirvāṇa.* Negatively, it is the annihilation of the notion of ego, complete negation of all egotism, of all desires, of the false view of substantiality of things etc.

As stated above, enlightenment or *nirvāṇa* lies in the effacement of the idea of individual self and in the cultivation of *anātmabhāva.* It is the widening of the self, the experience of '*aham brahmāsmi*' and '*tat tvam asi*' in the Upaniṣadic parlance. It is the expansion of the spirit of the individual and its merger with the universal. Śāntideva in Bodhicaryāvatāra gives a classical exposition of this state of existence as '*parātma samatā*' and '*parātma parivartana.*' He writes,

Parātmasamatām ādau bhāvayed evam ādarāt,

Samaduḥkhasukhāḥ sarve pālayantavyā mayātmavat. (8.90)

and,

Ātmānam cāparāṃś caiva yaḥ śīghram trātum icchati,

Sa caret paramam guhyam parātmaparivartanam. (8.120)

One who has the realization of *parātma samatā* and parātma parivartana will argue on the basis of parity that,

Mayānyaduḥkham hantavyam duḥkhatvāt ātmaduḥkhavat,

Anugrāhyā mayānye 'pi sattvatvād ātmasattvavat. (8.94)

Yadā mama pareṣām ca tulyam eva sukham priyam,

Tadātmanaḥ ko viśeṣo yenātraiva sukhodyamaḥ. (8.95)

Yadā mama pareṣām ca bhayam duḥkham ca na priyam,

Tadātmanaḥ ko viśeṣo yattam rakṣāmi netaram. (8.96)

i.e., "I should dispel the suffering of others because it is suffering just like my own, and I should benefit others because they are sentient beings just like myself. When both myself and others are similar in that we wish to be happy and do not want to suffer in any way, what then is special about me? Why should I protect myself and not others?"

The same idea is found to be expressed in several other texts. *Śikṣāsamuccaya,* for example, writes in a similar vein as follows:

Yadātmanaḥ pareṣām ca bhayam duḥkham ca na priyam,

Tadātmanaḥ ko viśeṣo yattam rakṣāmi netaram.

Under the impact of the doctrine of *karuṇā* the theory and practice of the traditional Indian theory of karma received a total transformation and instead of being mechanistic and retributive it became attributive and distributive. This modification was subsequently accepted by all non-Buddhistic Indian traditions. In the changed form it attributes the agency of karma to an agent but distributes the *karmaphala* to the society.[7] It, thus, advocates the transfer of merit (and of demerit as well) known as *pariṇāmanā.* In the *Bodhicaryāvatāra* we have a very impressive exposition of this phenomenon given by Śāntideva as follows:

Anena mama puṇyena sarvasattvā aśeṣataḥ,

Viramya sarvapāpebhyaḥ kurvantu kuśalam sadā.

i.e., ''Let all beings without exception be saved from sin and suffering on the basis of the merits acquired by me. Let everyone be happy on that account.''

He further writes,

Yat kiñcit jagato duḥkham tatsarvam mayi pacyatām,

Bodhisattvaśubhaiḥ sarve jagat sukhatamastuca.(10.56)

i.e., ''Whatever is pain and suffering in this world let it come to me. Let everyone in the world be happy on account of the good deeds of the Bodhisattva.''

Earlier he writes,

Evam sarvam idam kṛtvā yan mayā sāditam śubham,

Tena syām sarvasattvānām sarvaduḥkhapraśāntikṛt. (3.6)

i.e., ''Whatever good I have acquired by doing all this meritorious work, let it appease and assuage all the pains and sorrows of all living beings.''

The Buddhist ethical code springs from *karuṇā* and it touches each and every form of existence. The doctrine of *pratītyasamutpāda* as interdependence, interpenetration and interfusion of all phenomena, and the view of Dharmakāya as the unity of all existence in which "in one is all and in many is one. One is identical to all and many is identical to one"[8] provide a solid foundation for the Buddhist concern on ecology. The concern for the welfare of the natural world has been an important element throughout the history of Buddhism. Also the recognition that human beings are essentially dependent upon and interconnected with their environment has given rise to an instinctive love and respect for nature. The conception of Buddhist ecology has a global perspective: Love of and consideration for nature has been its cornerstone. The flow of *karuṇā* does not get arrested with human species but extends to nature.

The advocacy of universal responsibility in Buddhism has vegetarianism as its corollary. *Ahiṃsā* and *karuṇā* imply *sarvasattvānukampā* and *sarvajīvadayā*. It avoids killing of the life of animals and plants. All kinds of lives are sacred and meaningful. In the *Jātaka* stories we find that plants and animals speak to human beings. Meat eating and killing of animals or even cutting of green trees is a violation of the Buddhist spirit of *karuṇā*.

The Buddhist doctrine of *karuṇā* calls for a trans-valuation of values through a paradigm shift based on an enlightened view of life and reality. It calls for a global ethics of responsibility and mutuality. It advocates for the wholeness of life, the realization of infinitely complex networking of relationships, the living and working together in a group (*saṃgha*), the sharing of a common life with cosmic fraternity etc.

The Buddhist ideal of life has been very aptly described in the following verses quoted by Suzuki (p. 53):

Arouse thy will, supreme and great,

practise love and sympathy, give joy and protection.

Thy love like unto space,

Be it without discrimination, without limitation.

Merits establish, not for they own sake,

But for charity universal,

Save and deliver all beings,

Let them attain the wisdom of the Great Way.

The quest for perfection and attainment of excellence in life characterises the Buddhist scheme of trans-valuation of the values. Life is meaningful in pursuit of the ideal and not the actual. The meaningfulness of life consists in the gradual flowering and fulfillment of one's own being in cooperation with and through the help and support of other beings. Enhancement of the quality of life has been the perennial existential concern of all human beings. All human endeavors are prompted by and oriented towards this perennial concern. The traditional Indian concept of *puruṣārtha* is one of the prominent formulations of this concern for achieving quality of life.

The Buddhist view of life is opposed to the materialistic conception of life and human being. It goes beyond the materialistic confines and brings it into the wider consideration of the total human being. There can be no denying of the fact that food, clothing, shelter etc. are the basic necessities of life and they must be considered on priority. They constitute the base of human existence and therefore they are of foundational value. Any consideration on the quality of life must therefore begin with ensuring a minimum level for the standard of food, clothing, shelter and other basic material requirements. In the absence of these essential material things, human existence can be worse than that of an animal. But it should also be remembered that a human being does not live by and for the sake of these material things alone. There are deeper aspects of life which should be taken into account in any developmental program concerning the life of human being. There are different levels and states of human aspirations and achievements and in a holistic program of life all must find due place and importance.

In the Buddhistic conceptual framework no developmental program can be effective and enduring if it is one-sided, attending only just to the material or spiritual. The two need to be synthesised. Nāgārjuna, a great Buddhist thinker, has very perceptively stated in the Mādhyamika-kārikā (10) that:

Vyavahāram anāśritya paramārtho na dṛṣyate,

Paramārtham anāgamya nirvāṇam nādhigamyate.

i.e., ''Without having worldly knowledge the ultimate truth is not understood and without realizing the ultimate truth *nirvāṇa* cannot be attained''.

He further writes,

Na saṃsārasya nirvāṇāt kiñcid asti viśeṣaṇam,

Na nirvāṇasya saṃsārāt kiñcid asti viśeṣaṇam. (XXV. 19)

Nirvāṇasya ca yā koṭiḥ koṭiḥ saṃsaraṇasya ca,

Na tayor antaram kiñcit susūkṣmam api vidyate. (XXV. 20)

i.e., ''Nothing of empirical existence is different from nirvāṇa, nothing of nirvāṇa is different from empirical existence. That which is the status of nirvāṇa is also the status of saṃsāara. There is not the slightest difference between the two.''

So there should be synthesis of science dealing with *vyavahāra* and spirituality pertaining to *paramārtha.* Science alone, which is built on relative knowledge, is not able to satisfy all spiritual cravings, but it is certainly able to direct us in to the path of enlightenment.

Śāntideva in the *Bodhicaryāvatāra* pleads for universal progress and universal well-being. Every person must be able to manifest his/her capabilities through a dynamic discovery of one's potential for being assisted in this process by the society. No distinction can be made in this regard in terms of race, colour, creed, sex or country.

Going a step further and this is much more a concern of *karuṇā*, a special consideration must be given to the physically and/or mentally disabled people who are poverty-stricken. All is not well with the life of the disabled people in general and the poverty-stricken slum dwelling ones in particular. Apart from the fact that they have an intrinsic dignity and right to exist, and to unfold their capabilities in full, it is also a social obligation on our part to care for them and work for their welfare. In this respect no discrimination or compromise can be made between able or disabled persons as all have similar capabilities and similar goals to pursue and realize in order to live a meaningful life.. On the contrary, there should be a special display of *karuṇā*, a preferential treatment in view of their double handicap.

There is another point which must be emphasized in understanding the meaning and scope of the quality of life. It concerns the individual as well as the cosmos. Since the two are interrelated, interdependent and one organic whole, one cannot attempt to realize a good quality of life keeping in view an isolated individual, society, nation or region. It has to be a global vision and a universal realisation without any prejudice to any one section of the universe.

Notes

1 The word '*karuṇā*' occurs very frequently in all principal treatises of Mahāyāna tradition though it also occupies a prominent place in the Hīnayāna literature. *Karuṇā* stands for a very complex process comprising many types of feelings and hence no single word in English language can convey its full meaning. The Mahāvyutpatti discusses thirty two aspects of *karuṇā* writes Hardayal in "The Bodhisattva Doctrine in Buddhist Sanskrit Literature" (p. 24). It comprises all the *brahma vihāras, pāramitās* etc.

2 Suzuki points out that the term 'Mahāyāna' was first used to designate the highest principle, or being, or knowledge, of which the universe with all its sentient and non-sentient beings is a manifestation, and through which only they can attain final salvation (*mokṣa or nirvāṇa*).

3 The concept of Dharmakāya constitutes the central point in the Mahāyāna tradition. It is the highest principle in which the Buddhist find the ultimate significance of life.

4 The Buddhist literature abounds in stories, parables and legends pertaining to *karuṇā, tyāga, dāna* etc. exhibiting exaggerated philanthropy, self-denial, self-sacrifice etc. for universal welfare being undertaken by the Buddha and the Bodhisattvas.

5 Śāntideva writes: Mucyamāneṣu sattveṣu ye te prāmedyasāgarāḥ,Tair eva nanu paryâptam mokṣeāserikena kim. (XIII. 108) Ataḥ parārtho kṛtvāpi na mado na ca vismayaḥ,Na vipākaphalākāṃkṣā parārthaikānta tṛṣṇayā. (8.10)i.e., ''Will not the ocean of joy that would be there when all become free be sufficient for me? What am I to do with my liberation alone? Therefore even while performing altruistic deeds I should have neither self-conceit nor amusement. I should not have any desire for the fruits as I should long only for doing goods to others."

6 A Bodhisattva possesses ten *praṇidhānas* all of which flow out from *karuṇā*(See Suzuki, pp. 308-10 for details). Likewise all his reflections are directed towards *karuṇā*(Suzuki, pp. 369-71).

7 Insistence on there being no *'kṛtapraṇāśa'* and *'akṛtābhyāgama'* gave it a retributive form, leaving no scope for grace, mercy, help and cooperation. Further, it can not provide for a distinction between management of karma and management of *karmaphala* which need not be mixed up.

8 Quoted in ''Buddhism and Ecology," p. 16, edited by Martine Batchelor and Kerry Brown.

Concepts of *Karma* and ṣaṃsāra in Indian and Japanese Culture

Rewati Raman Pandey

I

Karma and *Saṃsāra* (rebirth) are two key concepts of Indian Philosophy. Except for the Cārvākas, these two concepts have been unanimously accepted by all other systems of Indian Philosophy. The Western philosophy or religions hardly recognize such doctrines though implicit references do occur here and there.

II

Man is a moral being. The behaviour of animals and functions of machines do not fall under the domain of morals. They are amoral. Even man is not responsible when he is compelled to act in a certain way either by external circumstances or by inner passions. If a person does something in a fit of passion, later on, he regrets and says, I was not myself when I did it'. In such cases the agent is blamed, not for what he did but for the irrational state in which he allowed himself to be in. Freedom is essential for morality. When a man chooses a course of action out of his own free will, then only he is ethically responsible. But do we experience such freedom of choice on what we will? Is the will really free or under fetters? Indian concept of karma offers a solution to the above problem. Popular mind identifies the word karma with fate and the concept of karma with counsel of despair. This concept is often quoted for indolence and inertia. But the truth of this concept is just the opposite. The concept of karma does not mean fatality rather it means the freedom of will. We often blame others for our misdeeds but the concept of karma says we must own our responsibility for all our deeds, good or bad. Moral life is not a chaos; it gives no room for chance. Moral order means that a man's actions of the past are responsible for his present state and his present actions will condition his future life.

The theory of karma is rooted in the *Rig-vedic* concept of *Ṛta*. *Ṛta* literally means 'course of things'. This conception seems to have been originally derived from the regularity of the movements of the heavenly bodies like the sun, the moon and the stars; also, the alternations of day and night and of the seasons. In the hymn its meaning is extended so as to cover not only uniformity of nature but also moral order. The Gods are called 'guardians of *Ṛta*'. They reward the good and punish the wicked. Varuṇa, the ethical god of the *Ṛg-veda* is the upholder of the physical as well as moral order. No man can escape his vigilant eye.[1] In the Brāhmaṇas where rituals dominate, *Ṛta* becomes a synonym for *yājña* or sacrifice. Thus the concepts of *Ṛta* and *Yājña* anticipate the theory of karma in so far as they imply that each action does bear its fruit.

A precise theory of karma is formulated only in the UpaniCads. Karma, here, means not only 'deed' but also the results of the deed. 'As we sow, so we reap'. There is conservation of moral values, just as there is conservation of physical energy. Nothing is lost which has been earned by work; and nothing comes in which is not earned. Every action has a double effect: it must produce its appropriate reward and it also should affect character. This aspect is very pertinent. While character informs conduct: conduct in turn moulds characters. A man becomes good by good deeds and bad by bad deeds.[2]

If the theory of karma is the counterpart, in the moral sphere, of the mechanical law of causality, where then is freedom? Modern science does not believe in the absolute determinism of the mechanical process. On the contrary, it admits that there is indeterminacy or uncertainty in nature. The past, no doubt, is happened and shaped; but the future is uncertain, not because of our ignorance but because of the very nature of the unpredictability of things in future. The causal law is not absolute and it cannot explain all things. If there is uncertainty and incalculability even in the realm of physical nature, then there must certainly be a greater degree of freedom in human nature. Karma does not bind man entirely. The cycle of *Saṃsāra* does not have the inevitability of a fate. Man has the freedom to go out of the vicious circle; and if he has the will. *Karma* will help and not hinder his progress. There needs to be a certain amount of determination; but it is not meant for the exclusion of all freedom. Radhakrishanan is very consistent: "the cards in the game of life are given to us. We do not select them. They are traced to our past karmas, but we can call as we please, lead what suit we will and as we play, we gain or lose. And there is freedom."[3]

The Aspects of Karma

The Hindu concept of *karma* has been derived into three kinds, *saṅcita, prārabdha* and *āgam*i or *kriyamāṇa.* Under the category of *sañcita-karmas* come all the accumulated karmas of the past. Part of it is seen in the character of the individual, his tendencies, and aptitudes; inclinations and desires etc. But their residues have not yet been matured, and therefore they have not yet begun to producing the consequences. Actions done in the previous life and the residues have matured to produce effects, have begun fructifying, i.e. producing the consequent results is called *prārabdha.* The Action done in the present life where there is a very thin maturation are called *sañciyamāna* or *kriyamāṇa* or *āgami.* The apt analogy that is usually given to explain the element of freedom in karma is explained as follows: Imagine a 'bowman' with a quiver of arrows, taking aim and shooting arrows at a target. He has already shot an arrow at the target; and another arrow is aimed at to be shot at the target by him. The bundle of arrows in the quiver on his back is the *sañcita*; the arrow he had shot at is *prārabdha*; and the one which he is about to shoot from his bow is *āgami*. Explaining this further, the shooter has perfect control over the *sañcita* and *āgamis* aspects, but on the *prārabdha* aspect of *karma* he has no control. Man has freedom to reform his character and alter his ways, but only with the past which already had taken place, he has to experience the consequent effects. The consequent effects of *sañcita* and *sañciyamāna* actions can be avoided with the attainment of knowledge, but those of the *prārabdha* actions cannot be changed by any means; 'only the fruits (results) of unripe *karma* can be destroyed by true knowledge'. Nothing accrues to the doer on account of his lost actions, and nothing accrues to him anything other than the results of his actions. The law, therefore, should be called the law of conservation of moral values. The law of conservation means that there is no loss of the results of the actions done (*kṛtapṛnasa*) and that there is no happening of events to a person except the results of his own actions (*akṛtābhyupagama*). The world which is governed by the rules of *karma* and these rules are said to be a moral need, since it is in this world one is sure to get what he deserves, is sure to enjoy or suffer what he ought to deserve. It is a casual truth that good actions (*śukla-karma*) lead to happiness and bad actions (*kṛṣṇa-karma*) to unhappiness.

III

Karma and Spirit

Despite the fact that this theory of *karma* is unanimously accepted in the Indian systems, there are two views regarding the importance of *karma*. According to one view, mainly of the Mīmāṃsakas, the highest goal of life could be attained by prescribed types of *karma*. But according to the other view, essentially that of the Sāṃkhya and Vedānta, the highest goal of life can be attained only after renouncing *karma*. The former view attaches importance of *karma* as the only means for achieving the highest goal, while the latter holds that the real essential nature could be realized only through knowledge and only very few are really fit for receiving this knowledge.

The concept of *karma* cannot be understood in isolation with the concept of spirit. *Karma* is not mechanical movement; it involves the notion of will or the capacity of choice from among all possible alternatives, i.e. doing or not doing or doing differently. This capacity of choice cannot be thought of without consciousness. On the contrary, a materialist cannot legitimately talk of *karma*. The concept of *karma* takes us to a sphere which, in the words of Kant may be termed as "the kingdom of ends", a non-material sphere or spiritual sphere. The concept of karma is associated with the capacity of an agency which by nature is willing an end, is something spiritual. Is it the essential nature of spirit to be active or to be a doer (*kartâ*), or is it only accidently happening? Here we have two conceptions.

According to one view, the agency necessarily belongs to the soul. This view is upheld by the Mīmāṃsakas and the Kaśmīra-Śaivism in India as well as different religions in the West. That is why *karma* is emphasized by the former Indian schools and morality by the latter Western religions. Here it is to be noted that in spite of their emphasis on morality and virtue they admit that salvation is granted only by God; it is purely with the Grace of God and not one's *karma*. However, so far as the dynamism of soul is concerned there is clear agreement between the two.

The other view maintains that the essential nature of spirit is it to be self-contained, because it is perfect. If karma is meant for achieving an end, and if spirit is perfect and motionless, then is it not as dead as matter? It can be replied with an argument that the spirit is the unmoved mover, but not the matter. Contextually, pure spirit in association with matter or under the condition of bondage seems to be active, though really it is not. In the Gīta, Krishna advises Arjuna: "There is nothing in the three worlds, O Pārtha, that should be done by Me nor anything unattained that might be attained."[4] "Man too thinks of himself as an agent only due to folly born of egoity."[5] Even God had to take birth in order to be an agent; he had to have associated himself with matter for an incarnation. Could God preach like Christ or annihilate Rāvaṇa like Rāma without having a recognizable human form? *Karma* requires a bipolarity which is considered as an essential characteristic of man; the aspiration that a human being possesses is not there, neither in the matter nor in the God. For instance, the aspects of *karma* are not functional in the vegetable world or in the animal world. Both these worlds are near to matter from the human perspective. *Karma* is possible only for a human being who has aspiration and has the ability to transform. This shows the spiritual significance of *karma*. Noted scholar Tripāṭhī's remark is very pertinent here: 'From the stand point of absolute spirit, capacity of karma is a fall while from the stand point of mineral, vegetable, animal kingdoms the capacity for karma is a mark of evolution, a relative detachment from matter. Hence though karma is possible only for imperfect it is a sign of going towards perfection.'[6] Contextually, schools like Kaśmīra-Śaivism adopts just opposite position: *Kriyā* is the essential nature of Parama-Śiva, and so also the Buddhist Vijñānavādins.

Karma requires an imperfect spirit or soul, but the idea of imperfect spirit appears to be self-contradictory. This aspect has a universal appeal. Both in India and the West the idea of imperfect spirit has been admitted. Indian systems remove the contradiction by suggesting that the imperfection in soul is only accidental and it can be removed by knowledge. But this contradiction persists in the Western religions like Christianity, because the imperfection of soul is taken to be its essential nature and real. Therefore, the soul can never attain perfection under any circumstance.

Karma is attributable to aspiration for something, and the attainment of which would lead to the cessation of *karma*; but, ironically, it is not so, because *Karma* can never achieve anything permanent. All the fruits of karma are impermanent, because everything that has a beginning has an end; even the attainment of *svarga* has only temporary existence. Man gets only temporary, if any, happiness, which succeeds in developing attachments (*vāsanā*). In fact, the frustration of desire for the permanent happiness together with attachment for objective things is the reason for rebirth. The souls conditioned by the attachment for material objects have to go through rebirths (*saṃsāra*) until they turn either to God or to the self in search of happiness. Here one thing is remarkable. It is not merely doing *karma* that gives rise to rebirth (*saṃsāra*) but the attachment to its fruits. The significance of *Niṣkāma-karma* of Bhagavadgītā, can be introduced here: it is as good as no karma; for Lord Krishna is never subjected to any bondage though he does *karma* as he has no interest in its fruits. (*na me karmaphale spṛhā*).[7] *Karma* with the desire for fruits would create two illusions: the illusion that the *karma* one does will surely produce the desired fruit, and the other illusion is that the fruit would make one happy forever. The Gītā advises us to get rid of both these beliefs. If the spirit seeks satisfaction from objective things, it is only due to its ignorance or illusion (*ajñānaṃ karma saṇginam*). In the case of Christianity the idea of this illusion could be considered as the original sin.

For the believer in God who is not a jñānī, i.e. who does not regard the world as illusory, there is apparent difficulty. Is it not a mockery that God should place man in such a position that while he has the urge or the capacity to do karma, it is neither in his power to get the fruits he wants nor is it in his lot to get permanent happiness from the fruits that he gets. To place man in such predicament does not reflect the goodness of God, yet it does. It is by experiençing frustrations repeatedly in achieving results that man learns that he is not the real doer and that some other power is at the helm of affairs. Man can realize his importance only by acting and failing. It is only by suffering that man can turn away from objects, and this is the Goodness of Lord. Thus the law of karma is nothing but immanent Divine Grace. It is not to be mistaken for the law of reward and punishment.

IV

Karma & *Saṃsāra*

The theory of *karma* is related to the conception of rebirth (*saṃsāra*) and of desire (*vāsanā*). It is the desire (*vāsanā*) for enjoyment of the fruits of *karma,* which binds the soul to objective things. If the concept of desire (*vāsanā*) is not admitted, then the reasons for both rebirth and birth cannot be explainable. Why the pure soul should take birth with a body of matter is only because of the basic illusion of desire (*vāsanā*). If the concept of desire (*vāsanā*) is admitted then we can explain the conception of birth and rebirth (*saṃsāra*) where rebirth becomes inevitable for the liquidation of desire (*vāsanā*). Indian religions which are all based on the concept of *vāsanā* and *saṃskāra*, have the doctrine of *saṃsāra* essential to them. This doctrine is not only organic to Indian Spirituality but also to its distinctive feature. The Christian teachings hold: "the idea that aeons are needed for the development of each individual man is one which is still foreign to the Western mind. A dominant Christian belief that one brief earth life can for a man the tremendous penalty of eternal damnation, is one of the accepted doctrines of all Christian Churches."[8]

Science has no clear explanations to the theories of *karma* and *saṃsāra*. These theories must remain as articles of faith for those who are not a yogi like Buddha, who are capable of seeing far into the past and into future. Such truths are revealed truths and so all that we should expect is that they should not be against human rationality, but not that they should be rationally proved.[9]

The theory of *karma* and *saṃsāra* has the merit of solving one great problem of the philosophy of religion, the problem which has been haunting the Western religions without giving any satisfactory solution. If God is all goodness and also all-powerful, then why is there so much evil and inequality in this world? Indian religions, contextually, relieve God from this responsibility; instead make the *karmas* responsible for inequality and evil. Western religions situate this problem to the will of God. Buddhism and Jainism do not even bother about introducing the idea of a creator and hold the view that this diversity in the world is attributable to our *karmas* (*karmajaṃ lokā vaicitryam*). Contrary to the views of Western scholars and Christian missionaries, the theory of *karma* and *saṃsāra* make man responsible and morality directed.

The doctrine of *karma saṃsāra* is therefore to be regarded as a part of the divine device to enable *jīva* to secure its salvation. This device works in many ways: by constant spiritual practices, the *buddhi* gets purified and truth will be reflected on it, which means the knowledge is born in the consciousness, and therefore the karmas are annihilated; or by experiencing repeated failures and frustrations, man with the Grace of God, comes to realize that he is not the real doer but some other power to whom he submits and surrenders helps him to attain his goal. Tripāṭhī's remark is very pertinent in this context:

> Life is not a mad man's dance. Even the Advaitin who subscribes to the theory of illusion, accepts the working of Divine Grace in the universe and believes that the world is a cosmos and not a chaos.[10]

I have no authoritative understanding of the Japanese concepts of *karma* and *saṃsāra*, however my humble reflection on it, in brief is: given that the work culture of Japan is excellent. Japan is the only country where economic prosperity and cultural advancement have been integrated, the Japanese can understand the implications of *karma yoga*. The concept of *karma* is ingrained into the psyche of Japanese culture. *Karma* is a 'leading doctrine of Japanese Buddhism'.[11] The Japanese socio-religious atmosphere is so surcharged with the karmic concept that when Japanese people encounter certain misfortunes they investigate into the causes and reasons. This philosophical orientation coupled with a superstitious tendency in Japanese thinking is the main explanation for the thriving business and of divination practiced throughout Japan.[12] It is not strange that in Japan when people encounter misfortunes they seek their explanations from religion.

It is taken for granted that *karmas* of former existence are relevant to one's fate in this life. It is also maintained that the blessings which are coveted may not be granted in this life. The new religions have accepted the Buddhist teaching of *karma* and its accompanying doctrine of past and future existence and it serves an important purpose in their teachings regarding sickness and healing. The concepts of *karma* and *saṃsāra* play a very significant role in the ethical life of Japanese even today.

Notes

1 ṚV. I.25.10, C. R. T. H. Griffith, *The Hymns of the Ṛgveda*, Benares, Lazarus & Co., 3rd ed., 1920-6.

2 *Bṛhadāraṇyākopaniṣad*, IV.4.5.

3 Rādhākṛṣṇan, *The Hindu View of Life*, p. 75.

4 *Gītā*, III.22.

5 Ibid, III.27.

6 Tripāṭhī, R. K., *Problems of Philosophy and Religion*, Center of Advanced Study in Philosophy, BHU, Varanasi, 1971.

7 *Gītā*, IV.14.

8 Edmond Holmes, *The Creed of Buddha*, p. 30.

9 Tripāṭhī, R. K., *Problems of Philosophy and Religion*, p. 108.

10 Tripāṭhī, R. K., Ibid., p. 109.

11 Clark B. Offner ! Th. D., *Modern Japanese Religions*, Twayne Publishes, INC, New York, 1963, p.129 (quotation of Hearn, Japan: An Attempt., p. 215).

12 Ibid., p. 130.

The author is indebted to R. K. Tripāṭhī's chapter on Karma and Rebirth of Problems of Philosophy & Religion for following the line of approach.

The Ritual of *Tai Pūsam* and the Role of *Pandāram* in Malaysia

— Interpretation of an Ethnic Ritual of the Malaysian Indian Community—

Shinji Shigematsu, Ph.D.

Abstract:

This paper attempts to analyze the implication of *Tai Pūsam*, a ritualistic festival of Tamil Hindu migrants in Malaysia. Here, I mainly focus on the process of *Tai Pūsam*, the dual functions of the *Pandāram* priest as an organizer of rituals for the Hindu members and for the staff of a plantation company; and the significance of the ritual in the context of socio-cultural aspects.

Most of the modern Tamil migrants went to the Malay Peninsula as plantation workers and urban labourers, and settled down there during the late19th and early 20th centuries. They brought (took, otherwise, Tamil migrants came to Malay Peninsula) with them several religious rituals and festivals of their native places in south India to wherever they settled down in Malaysia. Among them *Tai Pūsam* ritual (festival) was the biggest and the most important one for their religious identity. *Pandāram*, the non-Brahman priests, who also had migrated to the Malay peninsula, and had predominantly organized the *Tai Pūsam* rituals especially in the plantation areas where there were no Brahman priests.

Tai Pūsam had been acquiring significance continuously among the Tamil migrants to awaken the feeling of "Tamilness" and south Indian "Hinduness" by implementing the ritualistic activities. *Pandāram* as a *jāti* also contributed, in the process of the ritual as a coordinator between the Tamil plantation workers and the plantation company as the sponsor of the ritual in order to integrate the Tamil plantation workers into the plantation community. Thus, *Tai Pūsam*, an ethnic ritual could be effective both in religious and in social integration within the "closed society" of the plantation world.

1. *Tai Pūsam*: From a South Indian Ritual to the Tamil Ethnic Ritual

Tai Pūsam is one of the most popular ritualistic festivals in south India. It is being celebrated annually on the day on which the asterism *Pushya* (Cancer) presides in the Tamil month of *Tai*, falling in the months of January-February. This day generally comes on the full-moon day of the month. The planet *Brihaspati* or Jupiter is said to be the presiding deity of the asterism *Pushya*. The worship offered to the asterism *Pushya* is considered to have special merits, since the *Brihaspati* symbolizes wisdom, and the Hindus generally consider him to be the preceptor of the God, and one of the most important of the seven planets.[1]

While it is of astrological origin and significance, there are many other myths woven round it with its observance over the ages. The myth is mainly connected with Śivā and his son Subramaṇya. The story of Subramaṇya's birth relates that Lord Śivā had ceased to be a war leader and had taken to the ascetic life of penance and austerity. This left the gods leaderless and they began to fare badly in their battle with the *Asuras*. One of the *Asura* leaders, Taraka rose in power and became a great annoyance to the gods. The gods went to Brahma for seeking his assistance but all he could tell them was that when Śivā would get married and have a son, his son could destroy Taraka. So the gods conspired among themselves to distract Śivā from asceticism and to make him aware of the charms of Pārvati. Śivā developed a love for Pārvati and they were married. After some time Śivā gave the gods the germ of life which they tended and it grew up as a handsome boy. Śivā and Pārvati then brought up this boy until manhood. The gods implored Śivā that he should be sent to fight Taraka, the *Asura*. His mother presented him the invincible javelin (Tamil:*vēl*) and sent him to the battle. He defeated Taraka and killed him, thereby liberating the gods from the *Asura*'s oppression. According to a legend the day on which the *vēl* was bestowed on him was *Tai Pūsam*.[2h]

In south India the term of *Tai* actually means "green plant" or "young thing", and the month of *Tai* is thought to be very auspicious. Therefore, the *Tai* festival is obviously meant for children, especially the young girls.[3]

Subramanya (or Lord Murugan) was the name given to a deity originally of the hills in early Tamil literature. [4] Tamil people in south India, therefore, worship Murugan especially at the rock temples situated at the six hills in Azhagar kōvil, Tiruchendūr, Swamimalai, Tirutani, Palani and Tirupparankunram.

The God Subramanyan (or Murugan) was exceptionally popular among Hindu Tamil migrants in the Malay Peninsula during the British period due to his symbolic representation of youthfulness, growth and vigour. He is also the family-deity of the Chettiyār community whose influence still predominate the Hindu religious life in the Malay Peninsula. There are many temples dedicated to Subramanyan, and *Tai Pūsam* has been celebrated in many of these temples before Malay's independence.[5] It is well known that Subramanyan is worshipped and *Tai Pūsam* is celebrated in Batu Caves in Kuala Lumpur[6]. However, it is also a well known fact that there are same festivals in many places where Tamil migrants of every caste and origin settled down all over the Malay Peninsula. These festivals also could show some variations depending on the regional, social and economic conditions of the Tamil residents.

2. *Tai Pūsam* and Ritual Organizations

2-1.The Plantation Society: Social Setting of *Tai Pūsam*

We shall overview the situation in a plantation in the context of social and economic background of *Tai Pūsam* rituals.

Boh Tea Plantation is located in the Cameron Highlands in central Malay Peninsula. It occupies approximately 6,000 acres and is the largest tea plantation company in Malaysia in the 1980's.

The plantation area is virtually a sort of self-sufficient society. It is composed of 6 Divisions located along the hilltop. The residents of the plantation society have generally contact with the relatives and friends of the local towns within a radius of 30 to 40 km, and do not have frequent contact with the daily life of "outer-world" in the urban areas such as Kuala Lumpur, Pinang and other such big towns.

Of the population of 3,000 residents, more than 80 per cent are of South Indian Tamil people who belong to the first, second and third generation. The first generation of migrants came to this place around 1940's. According to the field survey conducted in 1980-82 by the author on the daily life and customs, it was found, that they continued to maintain the "traditional" norms and forms such as food habits, life style, costumes, hobbies, kinship relations, mutual assistance relations, language and the Hindu deities as those had been practiced in south India, for more than 40 years.[7] In this sense, the plantation society needed to preserve the south Indian tradition in Malaysia.

The South Division, one of the six Divisions of the plantation, has 52 households and 206 residents. Besides, there are Malay families (8 households, 30 persons) also there as community members, but no Chinese residents are living there.

The household numbers by the area of origin of South India, generations fist~Third of residents are shown in **Table 1** and **Map**. It is obvious that migrants came from almost every district of south

India, except Coimbatore, Tanjore and Chingleput districts; and 80per cent of them were from South Arcot and Salem districts.

In terms of *Jāti* composition, the South Division itself has13 Jātis. They are from the *Jātis* of *Goundar, Vanniyan Goundar, Padayachi* of agricultural occupation;, *Mudaliar; Āchāri* of craftsmen group; and other agricultural labourers like *Parayan* and *Nādār.* This composition is similar with a case of 16 *Jātis* of a village in Salem District in south India[8]. Among 13 *Jātis Velala Goundar* and *Vanniyan Goundar*, who are dominant in the inland districts of south India, are the majority in South Division (**Table 2**).

In terms of the economic and social function, we find that *Goundar* has the dominance over the functions as the Division Conductor and also as *Kangāni* in the plantation.

2-2.*Tai Pūsam*: Process of Ritual in the Plantation Society

The festival generally lasts three days in the tea plantation society at the Cameron Highlands.[9]

We shall trace the ritual process according to the time sequence from one year in advance before the festival on to the *Tai* day.

1) Collection of the funds for the festival, one year in advance before *Tai Pūsam* (**F**)

- The Temple management fund, from the monthly payment of plantation workers
- Donation from the Temple chit fund, "Kōvil Kuttu"

2) Maintenance of ritual places, from two months in advance before *Tai Pūsam* (**M**)

- Restoration of the temple and setting of the altar
- Cleansing the idol of the deity

3) Procurement of the ritual tools, from two months before *Tai Pūsam* (**M**)

- Assembling float, *Kāvadi* and other ritual decorations
- Borrowing the iron bars, silver hooks and silver strings for using at penance ritual

4) Maintenance of the procession route in the plantation hill areas, from ten days before *Tai Pūsam* (**M**)

- Road maintenance

5) Setting up of the common feeding camps, from ten days before *Tai Pūsam* (**M**)

- Carrying water, food and cooking fuel to the hill top temple
- Setting up the temporary dining hall

6) Preparation for common feeding, from ten days before *Tai Pūsam* (**M**)

- Preparing the cooking materials

7) Preparation for participating in the penance, since 42 days before *Tai Pūsam* (**R**)

- Avoiding the ritual im rity for 42 days by the penitents

8) Procession of the deity, Subramaniyan, on the day of *Tai Pūsam* (**R**)

- Carrying chariot with the deity along the route on the hill by penitents
- Carrying the *Kāvadi* by penitents
- Accompanying the penitents and devotees by chanting the slogan:

  "*vēl, vēl vetri-vēl*"("javelin, javelin Oh!, invincible javelin")

9) Presiding the rituals, on the day of *Tai Pūsam* (**R**)

- Hymning the Mantra by the *Pandāram*
- Firing the *Hōma kuṇḍa*

- Sacrificing of the animals
- Shaving off the hair of children
- Piercing children's ear

10) Common feeding and entertainment, on the day of *Tai Pūsam* (**R**)

- Dining by all participants disregarding *Jāti*, occupation and ethnic.

Note:

(**F**) means mainly financial procedures related to *Tai Pūsam*

(**M**) means mainly manual works related to *Tai Pūsam*

(**R**) means mainly ritual works

2-3. *Tai Pūsam*: Ritual Organizations

To conduct *Tai Pūsam* annually, at least three groups had been organized and functioned in the South Division in Boh plantation (**Chart**). They are as follows:

1. **Young Men's Association of Plantation Workers**
2. **Temple Management Committee**
3. ***Kōvil Kuttu*(Temple Chit Fund)Members**

2-3-1. Young Men's Association of Plantation Workers

This association is a volunteering group formed only by men of the age between 15 and 30. However, the numbers of men with membership in the South Division were only 16 in 1981, while female membership were permitted by amending regulations.

The common purpose of the association is to promote friendship among the plantation workers through social gatherings such as, reading and reviewing of Tamil novels and poems; enjoying together the Tamil movies and video films; and conducting football game. They get together on every Sunday and holiday at the Hindu temple compound on the hilltop.

Although this association aims at entertainment among membership, it also plays a vital role in implementing the ritual preparation for conducting *Tai Pūsam*.

When we observe each process of the ritual, we can find out about the division of ritual roles and secular functions by three groups of the plantation workers such as male full members, female semi-members, and senior members acting as consultants of the Association.

Male members contribute with their manual work especially to **the works at the stage of 2), 3), 4), and 5) of the process for ritual** as mentioned above: They repair the temple building; set up the altar; assemble the float and *Kāvadi;* maintain the road for the ritual procession; and carry the float on the *Tai Pūsam* day.

Young women prepare for **the works of at the stage of 6) and 10)** in the above process, such as, getting the cooking materials and the food items, cleaning the yard around the temple before *Tai Pūsam* , and cook and serve the food on the *Tai Pūsam* day.

Senior people also work **at the stage of 2) and 3)** such as borrowing the ritual tools like silver hooks, silver strings and long iron bars from the neighbouring Chinese temple. Every evening after work, they come together to the precinct of the temple and work together for *Tai Pūsam*. Such works continue for 10 days before the *Tai Pūsam* day. The senior Tamil people instruct the younger generation about Tamil customs, ritual procedures and traditions through sharing of the manual works and telling them about the Tamil heritage. .

2-3-2. Temple Management Committee

In the Boh Plantation there are three Hindu temples. One temple located in the Central Division where the head office and tea factories are located. It is managed and controlled directly by the company. Therefore, the plantation company supports the temple financially and employs the temple priests. Also, Temple Management Committee of each the Division manages of the other two Hindu temples located in the other two Divisions.

All Divisions of the plantation have the Temple Management Committees.[10] The committee is a non-profit and voluntary organization and is managed by five members. All the workers of Divisions, regardless of their occupation, *Jāti*, generation and native place in India, have the right to appoint the committee members. And any male persons can be appointed to the Committee as a member. And the duty is a part-time work and the title of membership of the committee is merely honour and not be compensated with any material benefit. In the South Division in 1981, the head of the committee was a tea plucker of Goundar caste. In this sense, the Committee is an autonomous body and a self-controlled religious and cultural organization. However, it has a close relation with the plantation management system of the company.

The main duty of the committee is the financial management of several rituals and to collect money for the Temple Management Fund for *Tai Pūsam* as **at the stage:1)**. Among these duties the most important work is the account keeping of temple fund which is compulsorily being deducted from the monthly payment of all of the plantation workers, and auditing of the *Kōvil Kuttu*. Besides these works, the Committee deals with accounting the cash money which was donated to the temple for the expenditure of the pūjas and *Tai Pūsam* festival; they also be selling the offered items, and paying monthly wages to the *Pandāram* priest. Thus, the committee has all responsibilities and rights on the financial matters related to the temple. However, all these procedures should be authorized by and managed through the company's management channel. Committee's functions cannot be effective without the permissions of the company. We shall observe this aspect in more detail in the following analysis.

2-3-3. *Kōvil Kuttu*[11]

Kōvil Kuttu is a sort of temple chit fund. It has two purposes. One is maintaining the rituals and another, is augmenting the mutual assistance system among the Tamil residents of each Division.

All plantation workers of each Division have to pay 1Malaysian Dollar (value: 50% of US Dollar inthe1980's) monthly to the plantation company's account as the ritual donation for *Tai Pūsam*. Financial section of the plantation company collects them and put them into an account of **Temple Management Fund**, and Temple Management Committee can manage and audit this account. In this sense, company with the authority has the right for collecting charity fund compulsorily from all plantation workers.

The numbers of workers are about 150 in South Division, and the annual capital of the fund came to be around M$1,800. Besides such regular and compulsory donations, it has annually an occasional income of M$1,000~1,500. These are the voluntary donations such as cash offered to *Pandāram* for *pūja* by the devotees, and the food items of rice, sugar, plantain, coconut, cloth and so on, besides cash offerings on the day of *Tai Pūsam*.

The Plantation Company also contributes annually a cash donation of M$1,000 to the charity fund under the name of supplementing the expenditures of *Tai Pūsam*. Thus, a total money of M$3,000~4,000 is the main source of the Temple Management Fund.

The *Pandāram* is paid monthly an amount of M$50/ (annually M$600/) from this Fund. And also the fund covers the expenditures for *Tai Pūsam* ritual, temple restoration and other purposes.

An amount of about M$800 is left after the ritual expenditures. This is used for giving small cash credit for all residents.

Any member of the South Division can borrow some small amount of money from the Temple Management Fund. Maximum amount that can be borrowed at one time is M$50 with 10 per cent annual interest. Most of the residential members of South Division are utilizing this facility of lending M$20 to M$30 as the allowed monthly amount from *Kōvil Kuttu*. The main purposes of this amount are living expenses (48 households), expense for *Tai Pūsam* (45 households), purchase of durable consumer goods such as TV, radio and kitchenware (37 households), medical expenditure (35 households), expense for visiting relatives in the towns (23 households), and also for consuming alcoholic drinks. Therefore, the *Kōvil Kuttu* is playing the vital role of supplementary living expenses for the plantation workers for maintaining their daily life in this closed society.

3. *Pandāram* Priest

Generally saying, there were a few Brahman priests available in most of the local towns and rural areas where Tamil or other south Indian migrants had settled, except in Kuala Lumpur. Instead, some members of *Pandāram*[12] as a *Jāti* performed rituals as priests in the south Indian dominated areas of the Malay Peninsula.

In the Boh Plantation area, all the priests in the Hindu temples of three Divisions belong to non-Brahman *Pandāram* priests. They perform almost all the Hindu daily *pūjas* and the annual *Tai Pūsam* festival for the residents who are of South Indian, Jaffna Tamil and Telugu Hindus. In South Division Mr. H., the *Pandāram* priest also performs all rituals and ceremonies.

According to the life history in the interview[13], when he migrated with his family to the Malay Peninsula around 1945, he was a member of the Indian National Army under Subash Chandra Bose. After the World WarII, he came to Cameron Highlands as a tea plucker and settled down there. At that time, there was no person to perform rituals for Tamil Hindu workers in the plantation, so he was requested to conduct occasionally the work as a part-time "priest". Since then the South Division and Temple Management Committee employed him as the full-time priest.

His duty as a priest includes daily *pūjas* in the morning and the evening at the temple, rituals of birth and naming of newly born children, ritual of ears piercing on the day of *Tai Pūsam*, and occasional rituals for puberty, marriage and funeral in the Division.

In the process of *Tai Pūsam* ritual, he is the key person especially in **the works at the stage of 1), 3), 7), 8), 9) and 10).** On the day of *Tai Pūsam* he chants hymn to make holy the rituals of birth and naming of the newly born and the ears piercing ceremonies. He chants Mantras in order to purify the iron bar and other ritual tools of *Tai Pūsam*. In the name of *Pandāram* the Temple Management also collects funds.

In this regard, *Pandāram* as the priest has a full ritual right and power in the south Indian Hindu community of the plantation society.

However, observing his role from another perspective, he is not necessarily regarded as a full-fledged ritual authority.

Firstly, he is a paid employee with a monthly salary of M$50 from the Temple Management Fund for his authority and implementation of the rituals for *Tai Pūsam*.

Although he can personally get cash and food items in kind from the residents of the Division for the personal *pūjas*, he has no full right to own and manage cash and other offerings donated to the temple deity. These donations are regarded as the incomes of the Temple Management Committee and not of the priest. Thus, the Committee regularly checks him on these "incomes".

Secondly, collection of Funds is requested in the name of *Pandāram*, but virtually it is given to the company's accounting section. The company authority can control the ritual and religious affairs through the fund-raising procedures on the south Indian workers.

Thirdly, he can preside over *Tai Pūsam* festival just by a sanction of the Plantation Company.

So the festival can be performed with the help of workers of the Divisions under the patronage of the Boh Plantation Company.

We can find that *Pandāram* is of a vital ritual power as the priest of south Indian Hindu community, but *Pandāram* as a fellow staff of the plantation society is controlled and regulated by the Temple Management Committee and the Plantation Company. Thus, *Tai Pūsam* in the plantation society can be performed jointly

by the multiple organizations and the division of functions of religious authorities, that is, *Pandāram* and the Murugan deity, volunteering organizations, that is, Young Men's Association and Temple Management Committee and managing and financial organization of the Boh Plantation Company.

4-1. *Tai Pūsam*: Change from Individual to Collective Motives

In terms of the ritualistic structure ritual form and the religious objective of *Tai Pūsam*, we find that it is motivated and conducted primarily by the personal devotion.

4-1-1 the Personal and Individual Motives

Personal motivation and direct devotion to the God Murugan encouraged people directly to participate in *Tai Pūsam*, and they had originally to conduct the penitence individually. Motivation of participation as a penitent was not for wishing and praying for the future fortune and luck, but for the individual gratitude to the good result due to the God's grace. Practical motivations were the token of each gratitude for curing the diseases, recovering from sickness or injury, safe delivery of the child. Prayers are given for achievements such as getting a job, winning entrance examinations, occupational promotions, marriages and so on. Individuals who got the good results express their gratitude to the God Murugan directly by the act of penitence on the occasion of the *Tai Pūsam* ritual.

From the viewpoint of God-devotee relation, *Tai Pūsam* is regarded as similar to Bhakti cult, which was purely religious individualism at the primary level.

4-1-2. from Individual to Collective Motives

However, motivation and intention were transformed **from individual to collective, practical to abstract, and specific to general.**

As mentioned before, anyone can join the ritual regardless of *Jāti*, sex, age, occupation, native place in India, residential place, and ethnicity or nationhood.[14] Although only the individual penitence could express the will of thanks by the pseudo-experience of tolerance of the God Murugan, relatives, neighbours and working folks of the penitent, or even any persons who pray and any unrelated persons came to entrust their gratitude to Him.

Some devotees and penitents expressed their gratitude for recovery from illness of some Tamil film hero in south India or winning an election of the Tamil politicians in Kuala Lumpur or in south India. Others showed gratitude to the God for the success of senior persons in the office or leading persons in the local community. Penitents play a role in charge of others or for even abstract matters[15] such as general happiness and global peace and security. Thus, *Tai Pūsam*, in this context, has flexibility and tolerance than any other personal Hindu devotion in terms of an ethnic ritual.

4-2. *Tai Pūsam*: Populist Ritual of the Ethnic Tamils

Babb Lawrence, a cultural anthropologist noticed the importance of *Tai Pūsam* as an ethnic religious festival in Singapore[16]. The main notions in his article can be summarized as follows:

"Firstly, migrants in such a multi-ethnic society of cultural and social factors as in Singapore (and Malaysia) seek for a strong integrated ethnic identity. As for Tamil and south Indian migrant workers, Tai Pūsam is the most important ritual for awakening the feeling of "Tamil-ness" and Hindu identity among Tamil migrants. In his context of cultural anthropology, "Tamil-ness" means complex affinity of Tamil language and south Indian ecological cultures."[17]

Secondly, God Murugan (Subramaniam), the sole deity of *Tai Pūsam* is a populistic and a concrete symbol of "Tamil-ness", "South Indian-ness"[18] and "Hindu-ness". Therefore, Tamil migrants can be aware of the sense of such feeling and identity directly through the pseudo-experience of the God Murugan.

Thirdly, both penitents and the followers accompanying the penitents can enjoy these experiences in the ritual process of *Tai Pūsam*. Experiences in the rituals are those of sharing the devotees' motives, direct and indirect participation in each process of the ritual, trust of their will to be the penitent, chanting and singing of hymn in Tamil language with the accompaniment of south Indian musical instruments, and especially a common feeding at the final stage of the festival. These activities could strengthen the identities of Tamil, and the feeling of an absolute equality of all participants in the ritual.

Babb Lawrence found a close interrelation between individuality of the penitence and the collectiveness of motivation in *Tai Pūsam* in Singapore. Thus, he claimed that the importance of such interrelation had greatly contributed to awaken the Tamil identity.

4-3. *Tai Pūsam*: An Institutionalized ritual

In the case of *Tai Pūsam* in the plantation society, we can even find out collective motivations. For example, eight young devotee workers and two senior persons explained their motivation of being a penitent. They were requested to "express thanks to God" on behalf of the persons of South Division residents, relatives in south India, and friends and relatives in other parts of Malaysia for their good health, good economic condition and peace. Penitents are expected, whether it is spontaneous or not, to play the role of the representatives at each level of the community, such as, working group in the plantation, living units of the South Division, group of relatives in Malaysia and remote native places of south India.

However, we notice another aspect of *Tai Pūsam*. When we focus on the organizations and process of *Tai Pūsam*, they are well systematized in the mechanism of company's managerial functions.

As explained in section 2, we can recognize that all the plantation workers become compulsorily and automatically members of the Temple Management organization. Implementing force of *Tai Pūsam* is a good combination of young male and female, and senior members of community, and the company's sponsorship. All the society members of the plantation can participate and enjoy themselves the ritual festivities. The company controls collection and expenditure of the fund for rituals through Temple Management Committee. Sanction of performing *Tai Pūsam* is under the company's authority.

The ritual performance shall be a vital factor to promote integration and unity among Tamil migrants of three generations in the closed society of South Division with fifty-two households. The major significance of *Tai Pūsam* as an ethnic ritual can be obviously seen in a plantation society in Malaysia.

Notes

1. Jagadisa Ayyar, P.V. (1920,1982 rep.), *South Indian Festivities*, .N.D.31-32.
2. Arasaratnam, S. (1966), *Indian Festivals in Malaya*, University of Malaya.13-14.
3. Brenda Beck, E.F. (1972), *Peasant Society in Kongu:* Univ. of British Columbia Press.:52-53.
4. Clothey Fred, W. (1982)", Chronometry, Cosmology and the Festival Calendar in the Murukan Cult" in Guy R.Welbon and Glenn E.Yocum (Eds.), *Religious Festivals in South India and Sri Lanka*. Manohar, 183.
5. Arasa ratnam, S. (1966): 15.
6. In Kuala Lumpur Tai Pūsam is presided only by Brahman priests in the Mahā Māriamman temple in the central area.
7. Shigematsu Shinji "Migrants' Society and a Multiple-Network: A case of BohPlantation (Iminshakai to Fukugou Network)" in *Historical Sociology of International Migration* (Kokusai Idou no Rekishi-Shakaigaku). Nagoya University Press.1999.
8. Shigematsu Shinji "Integration and Transformation of a South Indian Village of Migrants (Imin-boson no Sonraku-tougou to Hennyou) in op.cit.

9. Participating observation by the author, from January 5 to February 10, 1981.

10. The residents of the Divisions, which have no temple, join the Hindu temple near their Divisions.

11. In Tami ***Kovil*** means temple and ***Kuttu,*** assembling or combining. In Japanese *Yui or Moai (or Tanomosi-kou)* has the same meaning and function.

12. Pandāram as a caste in south India is to be out of non-Brahman higher caste origin such as Velāla or Palli. (Thurston, E. *(1975*;1909), *Caste and Tribes in Southern India.vol.6.*). Their traditional occupations were considered to be those of festival cook, local priest, flower-tier, and eating-leaf provider (Beck: 305). In south India the Pandaram generally presides the common rituals including the funeral ceremony which Brahman never do.

13. Shigematsu Shinji (1984), *Interview Documents of Overseas South Indians in Malaysia, Singapore and South India*, School of Letters, University of Nagoya, Japan.

14. In 1981, a few Chinese Malaysians and a few Europeans among 2,450 devotees participated in Tai Pūsam.(*Asiaweek*, 6, February, 1981)

15. We do not know whether the collective motivation and broader tolerance was conspicuous only in Tai Pūsam in Malaysian Indian community, or in south India too. And also we can not identify the period of transition when personal and practical motives were changed into non-personal, collective and abstract ones.

16. Lawrence, Babb (1980) "Tai Pūsam in Singapore: Religious Individualism in a Hierarchical Culture" *Asean Sociology* 14.

17. He claims Tamil culture as a sort of ecofest, which is based on specific ecological conditions and folk legends in south India.

18. There is a delicate marginality between Tamil-ness and South Indian-ness. The former concept is in this context based on the cultural value of Vellala-dominated society in Deep South India. On the other hand, the latter includes the multiple cultures and social norms of Tamil, Malayalee, and Kannada.

Table 1: Numbers of Family by Place (District) of Origin and Generation.

23 families from South Arcot(Ⅲ=16, Ⅱ=6, Ⅰ=1)

18 families from Salem(Ⅲ=2, Ⅱ=10, Ⅰ=5, Unkonown=1)

3 families from Pudukottai(a part of Tiruchy) (Ⅲ=2, Ⅱ=1)

2 families from Dharmapuri(Ⅱ=2)

2 families from Tirunelveri(Ⅲ=16, Ⅱ=6, Ⅰ=1)

1 family from North Arcot(Ⅱ=1, Ⅰ=1)

1 family from Tiruchy(Ⅲ=1)

1 family from Ramnad(Ⅲ=1)

1 family from Madurai(Ⅱ=1)

(Surveyed in 1984 by Shigematsu)

Note:

Ⅰ, Ⅱ, Ⅲ=Generation

1～16=Number of Household(s)

Map: Family Numbers by Place (District) of Origin and Generation

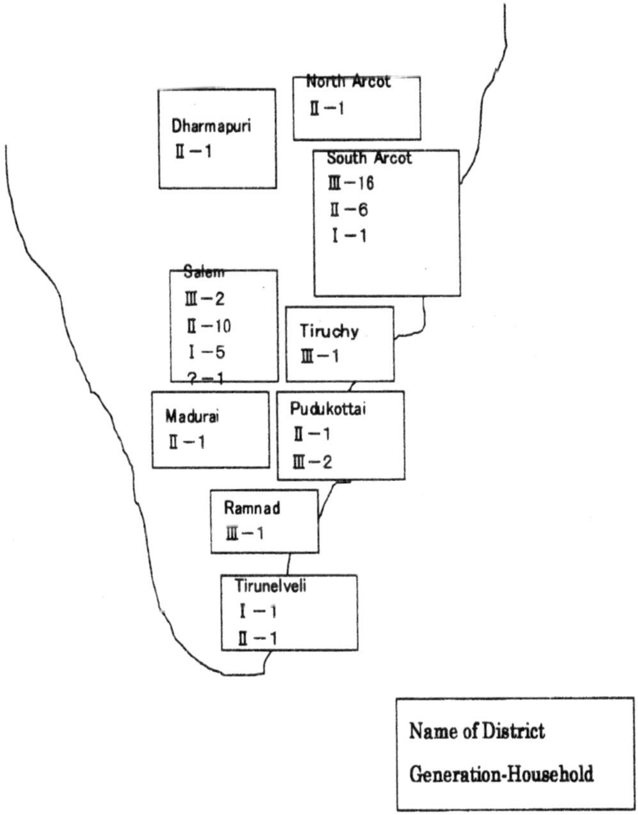

(Produced by Shigematsu)

Table 2: Jati and Occupation of a Tamil Community in Boh Plantation

Occupation → Jati ↓	DC KG	TP	GC C SW	DR	P	TD	SD	SO	F	RE	Total
G	3	9	1	1					1		15
VG		9	2							2	13
PD	1										1
PA	1	5	2								8
M	1										1
A		3	1								4
B		1									1
N		2								1	3
NC							1				1
C		1									1
T		1				1					1
K		1						1			2
P					1						1
Total	6	31	6	1	1	1	1	1	1	3	52

No. of Family in a Division of Boh tea plantation in Central Malaysia

<Occupational Functions in a Plantation Company>

DC=District Conductor, KG=Kangany, TP=tea plucker, GC=grass cutter, C=contracor, SW=sweeper, DR=lorry driver, P=Pandaram, TD=taxi driver, SD="Small Doctor"=male nurse, SO=shop owner, F=farmer, RE=retired person.

<Jati in a south Indian village>

G=Goundar,VG=Vanniyan Goundar,PD=Pandāram,PA=Paraiyar,M=Mudaliyar, A=Āchāri,B=barber,N=Nādār,NC= Nādār christian,C=Christian,T=Tēvar, K =Kallar, P=Padayachi.

(Produced by Shigematsu)

Chart: Pandāram, Plantation Company and Workers in Ritual Process

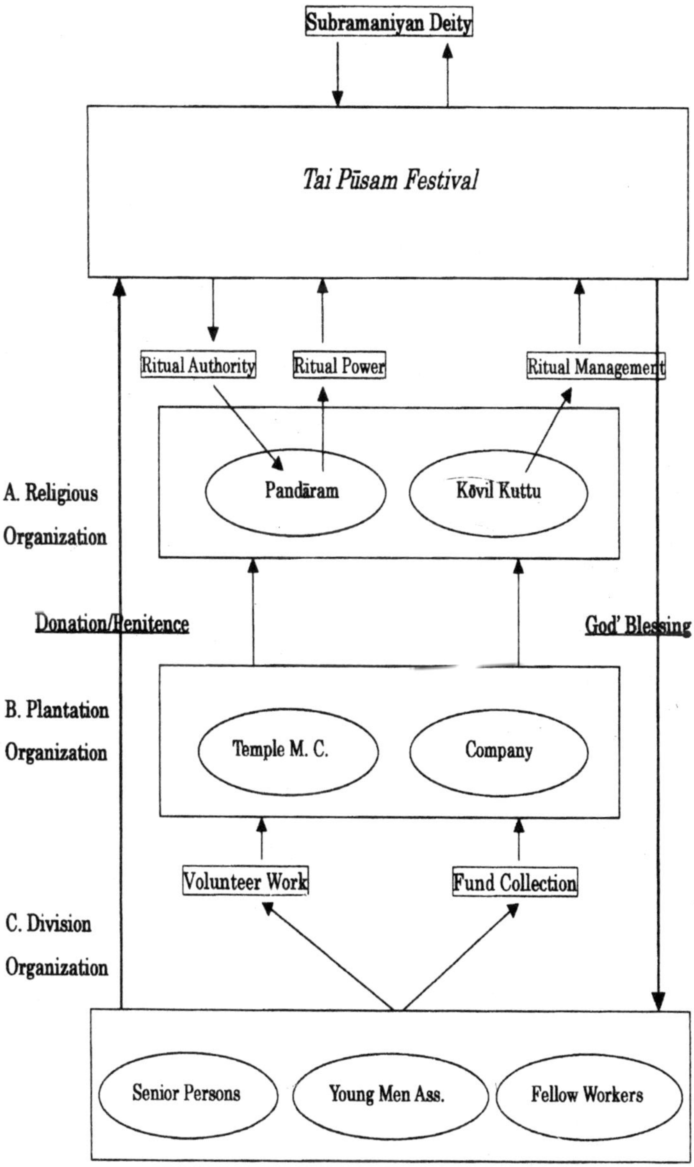

The Revival of the Buddha in Narratives:

The Conflict between Philology and the Science of History[1]

Masahiro Shimoda (University of Tokyo)

1 Philology and Historical Science: What is Suggested by Nakamura Hajime's *Gotama Buddha*

When scholars describe the history of Buddhism, they usually structure their narrative on the basis of the category of the three Buddhist treasures, the Buddha, the Dharma, and the Saṃgha. To attempt an overview of Buddhism from this standpoint, which has continuously given Buddhism at any time and in any place its foundations, sounds reasonable.

However, in dealing with these three categories, we notice an odd tendency in the approach of present-day scholars particularly in Japan: when dealing with materials concerning the Dharma (the teaching) and the Saṃgha (the community), they utilize all the available materials that refer to these two categories. When it comes to studies on the Buddha, however, the scholars, without giving concrete explanations of their methodology, divide the related materials into two groups: those that concern the history of the Buddha and those that deal with his legends. On the basis of these stipulations, scholars tend to go even farther to judge that the former deserves to be examined but the latter should be excluded from the scope of research.

It is difficult to specify exactly when this trend has started in Japan, but it may be safe to assume that this peculiar attitude of the Japanese scholars in dealing with research materials related to the Buddha was firmly established based on the influence of Nakamura Hajime's *Gotama Buddha*, (Shunjūsha Publishing, 1964, revised and published later as part of *The Best Selections of Hajime Nakamura's Works: Gotama Buddha*, I and II, 1992).[2] Nakamura, in trying to distinguish between the "historical" Buddha and the' "mythologized" or "deified" Buddha to single out the corresponding descriptions that could only extract the historicity of the Buddha, declared that he would exclude them from his scope of the materials and descriptions that do not meet this requirement.

However, in sharp contrast to its theoretical simplicity, this argument is very difficult to carry out at the level of practice. In fact, Nakamura was never consistent in applying this methodology to his researches in this book. The question of how to evaluate the *Gotama Buddha*, which has had enormous influence on the studies of Buddhism in Japan, is a focal issue to those involved in the study of the Buddha. When seen from the standpoint of "philological study," there is no doubt that this publication has made an enormous contribution by virtue of its abundant amount of information, but if the book, as the author claims, is viewed from the perspective of "historical study," the *Gotama Buddha* that lacks methodological consistency and its accompanying mode of discourse is due to be subjected to judicious criticism. A history to be reconstructed manifests itself in accordance both with the methods for the selection of materials as well as with the style of combining and presenting the selected materials.

It is its methodology and its descriptive style that set the *Gotama Buddha* quite apart from a historical investigation. In this book, Nakamura, in fact, arranges various kinds of materials extracted from primary sources, with his own comments added to them, yet without these two layers of descriptions united in a single context. It is not a style that describes "a history," but an approach providing raw materials in the form of fragments along with annotations, in a sort of "notecard style."

To establish a study that can be regarded as describing the life of a historical person, *Gotama Buddha* is colored with adequate characteristics; for Nakamura needed to have consolidated the fragments of almost all kinds of Buddhist materials, not only accounts belonging to the Vinaya and Sutra categories along with their commentaries, but also the stories of the Buddha, which the author had initially declared that he would not accept. The promise the author stated at the beginning of the book, that he would adopt a method of distinguishing between the "historical Buddha" and the "Buddha that has become a legend" to extract only the former from the extant materials, is ignored here. After having adopted almost all the materials as the sources to reconstruct the historical Buddha, Nakamura added a critique of them as an *ex post facto* report.

If one compares the attempt of reconstructing the "historical Buddha" by choosing appropriate materials from among the existing ones to the style of completing a jigsaw puzzle, the *Gotama Buddha*, which is tinged with this sort of peculiar style, cannot be seen as a completed jigsaw puzzle; it may be said to be a box of pieces labeled "the Buddha's life," in which the pieces necessary for the description of the historical Buddha, those unnecessary for it, and a huge number of pieces that are difficult to tell whether they are necessary or not, are all just placed, with 'Post-It' notes attached to each of them.

One of the main problems concerning the studies on the subject of the Buddha to date is that of the excessively high evaluation of the *Gotama Buddha* by scholars in Japan. Most of the Japanese Buddhist scholars, overwhelmed by the rich volume of information, have unconsciously taken this book as one that depicts the "historical Buddha," though the book in fact is nothing more than a box containing a vast number of puzzle pieces attached with dockets. This misunderstanding has, then, prevented scholars from recognizing the necessity to proceed to the next step of critical assessment of the actual findings by this study. The failure to do this has brought us to the current situation of academic studies of the Buddha, that is, the vague division of related materials into those that deserve to be examined and those that to be excluded.

It is true that the breadth and depth of Nakamura's work in terms of information provided towers so high that a good many subsequent scholars shied away from dealing with this topic. Beneath the lack of awareness on the part of scholars for the necessity of reevaluation of the *Gotama Buddha*, however, lies the lack of awareness of the significance of 'the variations of a descriptive style' according to each particular field of scientific inquiry. The lack of awareness of this aspect, then, exacerbates the ambiguity of the goal that the scholars of Buddhist studies are to pursue. Scholars should have been aware, from the outset of their studies on the topic of the Buddha, that there are at least two distinct spheres in which they should have focused their attention, either the historical science or the philology, and that each one of these two is to be constituted by its own descriptive style. The descriptive style adopted in the *Gotama Buddha*, which, as mentioned earlier, is nothing more than a collection of research materials with annotations, seen from the viewpoint of historical studies, is far from satisfactory. The same style, viewed from the standpoint of philology, however, does not seem to present any particular problems, for philology is a sort of basic study, of which the main purpose is to provide necessary and accurate materials to complete and criticize historical studies.

Seen this way, it is evident that the problem with the study of the Buddha initiated by Nakamura originates in an uncertainty, for which mode of inquiry should take precedence in Buddhist studies: *historical science* or *philology*. Buddhist studies, of course, allow us to go along either path, or both at the same time. What should be kept in mind, however, is that each of these two paths has its own destination.

Furthermore, it should be noticed that the issue proposed by the *Gotama Buddha*, when considered more deeply, is concerned with two questions: first, what is "Buddhist studies as a historical science"; and second, on the condition that Buddhist studies developed from philology to historical science, what is the "historical Buddha" that results from the science. To pay due attention to the intellectual history of twentieth century, in which more and more reflection has been given to the reevaluation of the science of history, one would find that Buddhist studies has sacrificed significant issues in exchange for its adherence to the notion of the "historical Buddha." Prior to elaborating on this subject, we will start with reviewing current studies of the Buddha that are excessively oriented in the single direction of the "historical Buddha."

2 Studies of the Buddha in the West

For a scholar that claims his or her study to be regarded as the history of science to simply exclude the historical materials that refer to the Buddha from the scope of research right at the start of the study, without examining any other possible modes of interpretation of them, would be too bold an attempt to accept. Before resolving oneself to such a crucial set of principles in terms of approach, one should resolve the problems with the related historical materials by considering every possible methodological option to the study of the Buddha.

Buddhist studies to date, however, has not displayed any convincing evidence for prioritizing any specific method of research concerning the historical Buddha. On the contrary, looking at the history of Buddhist studies in the West in modern times, it is evident that the figure of the historical Buddha reconstructed from the extant materials is one of the most seminal controversies. Buddhist studies is still at a developing stage in which basic methodologies should be carefully discussed. It would be of some help to trace back a little through the history of the study to elaborate on this topic.

Buddhist studies in Europe can be seen as having their start with the "discovery of the historical Buddha" in the early nineteenth century, and they continued to carry controversies concerning the entity of the Buddha among prominent researchers up until the mid-twentieth century. These two opposite poles of research, which, combined together, formed the foundation of Buddhist studies in Europe, provide an extremely useful suggestion in considering the issues of how to deal with extant materials and how to reconstruct historical facts.[3] At this point, it is simply a mystery that the *Gotama Buddha*, a book covering a tremendously vast amount of information from so many works of the East and the West from all time periods, does not mention this "debate on the entity of the historical Buddha" any place in the book.

Europe in the nineteenth century underwent radical changes in the study of Buddhism. Among other things, we should notice that Buddhist studies had not existed before this century in the strict sense of the word, for the term "Buddhism" was only created around the year 1820, with the historical Buddha as the main implication of the term contained. The notion of the Buddha, the central figure in the idea, however, was depicted mostly based on speculation with the help of a small number of historical materials. The fact that Western scholars at one time in history had attempted to establish the origin of the Buddha in Ethiopia, a fact often referred to as an ideal example of the difficulties in specifying the historical Buddha, shows how chaotic and difficult it was for those in Europe to understand a foreign culture that had been born far and away from their time and place.[4]

Researches based on historical materials gradually followed the above-mentioned discussions founded on speculations. This was made possible by the acquisition of materials concerning the Buddha's life stories. The work that appeared prior to all the other legends of the Buddha was, presumably, *Life or Legend of Gotama: Burmese Buddha*, an old Burmese legend translated by Paul Begundate in 1858. Following this work Philippe Foucault's *Lalitavistara: The History of Sakya Buddha in Tibetan Legends*, published in 1860. After the publication of Fausbøll's *JAtaka*, edited and published in 1877, several important translations or studies on the Buddha's life story were published one after another, such as Rhys Davids' *Legends of the Birth of Buddha or Jātaka* in 1880, Samuel Beal's *Romantic Legends of Sakya Buddha* in 1885, Leon Fehr's *Avadāna Jataka* in 1891, and James Grey's *Magnificence of Buddha by Jianālankāra or Buddharakita* in 1894.[5] As the appearance of these works shows, most of the stories of the Buddha became available after the mid-nineteenth century, and started to serve as invaluable materials to describe "the historical Buddha."

It should be noted that a once-settled debate over the historicity of the Buddha flamed anew in the midst of the development of these studies. The resumption of this debate was initiated by the French Indologist Emile Senart.[6] The point brought up by Senart was completely different from the doubt about the Buddha's historical presence that had been maintained before the nineteenth century when scholars did not even have a notion of "Buddhism." Senart argued that the more closely he examined the legends of the Buddha such as the *Lalitavistara* and the *Māhavastu*, the more evident through the descriptions of the Buddha was the structure of stories surrounding the world of Indian gods, and not the historical reality. His argument was fully an academic one, accurately based on relevant historical literature.

Buddhist scholars in Europe at the time were divided into two opposite camps concerning Senart's assertion. Among those who supported his view were Hendrik Kern in Holland and Max Müller in Britain, the latter of whom, rather exceptionally as a British scholar at that time, showed broad interest in Indian religions as a whole, not being at all limited to discussions of the issues of the historical Buddha. Representative scholars of those who remained against Senart's position, on the other hand, were Hermann Oldenberg and Mr. and Mrs. Rhys Davids. Arguments on both sides brought forward by these leading scholars were succeeded by Edward Thomas and Alfred Foucher up to the mid-twentieth century.[7]

What was actually at stake in the series of controversies is, to summarize briefly, a fundamental difficulty to define a historical existence by using the extant literary materials as proof. Oldenberg and Rhys Davids, who continued to support the verifiability of the historicity of the Buddha, in fact, assumed *a priori* the existence of the historical Buddha, and did attempt to prove his existence based on these materials. The main point of the assertion by the scholars who were skeptical of the plausibility of the reconstruction of the historical Buddha was, simply put, related to the matter of the overlap of a *history* with a *story*. A *history* must take the form of a *story* once it is completed, whereas not all stories are histories. By the way, all the descriptions currently available about the Buddha are in the form of *stories about the Buddha*. The issue at stake here, therefore, is how to make a distinction between the accounts of histories and those of fictions.

A given story could be called a history when the story satisfies the following two conditions: first, if the date and the place of the story are specified, and, second, if the story is proved to be connected exclusively to an identifiable and lasting trace left in the world. [8]According to Senart and Kern, there was no reason that the stories concerning the Buddha should be regarded as being attributed only to the particular existence of the Buddha Śākyamuni, but, on the contrary, they can be naturally seen as stories that relate themselves to other types of stories, such as the myth of the sun. To adduce the depiction of the Buddha's birth as an example, the bodhisattva Śākyamuni, legendarily a descendant of the solar god, comes down from the TuCita Heaven into the womb of a queen named Māyā, who doomed to die soon after the bodhisattva comes out of her wômb into the world. This series of events concerning the birth of the Buddha exactly matches with the episode embedded in the Vedic religion that describes the sun coming out of the earthly darkness, Māyā, by dispelling her.

When this sort of a fundamental question is put forth to the existing stories of the Buddha, it seems to be difficult to give an answer with any certainty. It is true that philological investigations often succeed in revealing a chronology of events within a text, but it cannot prove that any particular event drawn from the text is related to an event outside the text. At the same time, being unable to prove the historicity of the Buddha does not mean that his historicity is denied. Given the overlap of the story of the Buddha's birth with the myth of solar god, this concordance neither supports nor denies the historicity of a particular individual. If one cannot prove the occurrence of an event, one cannot declare that it never happened. In short, philology and the science of history do not always provide mutual confirmation.

Regardless of the above-mentioned methodological limitation, if the Buddhist scholars still have much concern about the historicity of the Buddha, the best solution to this issue would be to decide which one approach of the following two sounds more reasonable that has been shown in the introduction of *The Life of Buddha as Legend and History* by Edward Thomas. In front of the various traces of Buddhism exhibited all over Asia during the long course of history to date, which approach should one chose, to find the realization of a myth that initially lacked of historical reality, or to see a mythical or legendary development originally based on a historical event? To properly answer this question, we need to liberate our attention from the confines of the narratives of texts to the external world of such as sacred remains and Buddhist institutions, and ask in what manner the emergence of the Buddha, a particular historical event, should reasonably be located in these contexts. If a particular historical figure had not existed, then when and why Buddhist stūpas, art, rituals, the systems of their practice, and, more than anything else, Buddhists themselves, would have started to exist, and with the notion of a historical figure that died at the age of eighty cherished as their central figure.[9]

A simple answer to these questions may be that a historically important figure must have existed at the very beginning of the development of the Buddhist world, and, in the course of passing down through generations, the events surrounding the historical figure in the form of narrative gradually developed into magnificent stories involving natural phenomena and even the views on the universe. This assumption would seem more plausible when considering the fact that most of the events that have happened in the life of the Buddha are sometimes far from being commensurate with the traditional values of ancient Indian orthodoxy.

What should be borne in mind at this point, however, is that the question about the Buddha's historicity is not a question about being simply true-or-false, but a question fit to be dealt with by the basic awareness that one sounds more plausible as an explanation than the other. The discussion conducted in the nineteenth and twentieth-century Europe about the Buddha's historicity expressed a radical concern with the issue of how an event inside an extant text could be related to a historical event outside of the text. The debates, carried out for more than one hundred years, reached the point that the effort to clarify the Buddha's historicity based on the interpretations of references in the extant texts would end in vain. Not a few Buddhist scholars have endeavored to reconstruct an image of the historical Buddha by stratifying the chronological orders in different passages of a text, or from different texts by comparing them. It must be noted, however, that this approach does not go beyond the history of texts, and does not refer to any historical events outside the territory of the texts.[10]

3 Reconstruction of the Buddha's Personality: From History to Fiction

Most of the researches of the topic of the Buddha, especially outside the academic circle in the nineteenth- and twentieth-centuries of Europe, however, turned to a direction to define and evaluate the characteristics of the Buddha, paying no attention to the above-mentioned methodological issues. What is most striking in this method is that when Buddhism gained a reputation as a noble religion — second only to Christianity — all of Buddhism's advantages were attributed to the personal "characteristics" of the historical Buddha, and quite a few authors devoted themselves to depicting the Buddha from this standpoint. Raynold Copleston, Bishop of Calcutta, writing in anonymity, affirmed that it was "something in the personal gift of Gautama: his charm, his tact, his tenderness, the union of the sage with the friend, not anything in his discovery or in his institution, which gave him so vast and abiding an influence."[11]

These remarks by Copleston, to be rephrased from the viewpoint of the "three treasures," contends that the significance of Buddhism consists in the Buddha himself, or more precisely, the personal characteristics of the historical Buddha, not in the Buddha in the legendary form, let alone in the Dharma he discovered, or in the Saṃgha he formed. Given the decisive tone with which this assertion is made, along with its lack of proof, there lies underneath a sort of unspoken agreement of veneration of the founding religious figures.

In fact, religious authors in Europe at the time of nineteenth century shared a view that the Buddha, the founder of Buddhism, was the greatest figure imaginable, whereas Buddhism, as it had developed in Asia, became considerably corrupted from its assumed pure origins. According to David Armstrong, the teachings of the Buddha had been distorted into weird or grotesque absurdities, but what remained indelibly was the personality. He continues:

> That personality has endured this score of centuries, and is as fresh and beautiful now when displayed to European eyes, as when Siddhartha himself breathed his dying breadth in the shades of Kuśinagara. As in Christianity, so in Buddhism, the personality of the founder has been the only thing unchanged in the whirl and struggle of the ages.[12]

This remark by Richard Armstrong simply and clearly shows that the Buddha has existed in the world unchangeable and pure, though his teachings, the Dharma, and community, the Saṃgha, change, or deteriorate, over the course of time.[13]

It may sound natural to go on to investigate and evaluate the Buddha's personality once the framework of the historical Buddha is established by the studies of the Buddha. However, this procedure, in fact, results in the conflation of the ideal image of the Buddha with what the Buddha historically was. Instead of precisely observing the method of research, scholars, when dealing with the concept that represents the ultimate value of the research object, often fail to distinguish the ultimate sense value of their own from that which has to be the object of research. What Steven Collins has pointed out as the problems with the modern studies of nirvāṇa could precisely be applied to the studies of the historical Buddha.[14]

Among several leading figures who have pointed out this shortcoming as a theme of the history of Buddhist studies in the West, in modern times, Phillip Almond and Roger-Pol Droit would be worthy to mention. Their studies show that discussions concerning the Buddha and Buddhism were virtually conducted over the issues of Western thoughts; its religions, and its social problems discussed under the façade of Buddhism, reflecting the problems of the intellectual world of nineteenth-century Europe more or less related to the Christian thought. Most notably, the sharp contrast between the "corruption of Buddhist communities" and the "noble purity of the Buddha, the founder" is an exact reflection of the understanding of Christianity, usually common to the Protestants who were promoting the studies of the New Testament, declaring the "corruption of the Catholic Church" vs. the "purity of Jesus the Founder."

This is not, however, an issue confined to the European world in the past. Whoever tries to answer the question of what sort of person the Buddha cannot be but reflect the image of their own making as an ideal figure, as did the religious authors in the nineteenth-century Christian circles. This is solely due to the restrictions inherent in the relevant materials.

The literature on the Buddha, in the first place, must be distinguished into two types: one that tells about "what he said" and the other which relates to "what was said about him." There is no doubt it is the latter that describes who he was. The latter, however, within the purview of narratives that, starting with the impressions of the Buddha's disciples had on the Buddha, developed into various sorts of episodes during the process of dissemination. There is no guarantee in this process that the Buddha was objectively depicted. To evaluate his characteristics in the contemporary socio-religious contexts, the difficulty of reconstructing the historical Buddha on the basis of the stories of him taken into account, would be almost impossible.

On the other hand, an attempt to find out the historical Buddha on the basis of the former type of literature concerning "what he said," would be a similar attempt of identifying what a teacher really was like based on what he or she had given in verbal activities. This approach cannot always be justified. Nakamura may have been right when he asserted that such texts as Pārāyanavagga or Atthakavagga in the *Suttanipāta* or Sagāthavagga of the Saṃyuttnikāya could go back to early days of Buddhism, but these materials belong in the category of "what the Buddha said," and while these can well be taken to reflect the content of the Buddha's teachings; they cannot be taken as sources for knowing the events of his life and his characteristics.

In addition, given the fact that the Buddha's words and teachings were passed down at the early stage of the history of Buddhism only through oral transmission; their message must have been confined to the characteristics of this particular medium, especially in terms of vocabulary and style, and the uniqueness of Buddhism was all the more likely to be clouded with it. In this respect, not only the Buddha but also his teachings would be difficult to restore.[15]

If researchers still want to depict the characteristics of the historical Buddha under these limitations, they would have to go beyond the realm of historiography, transgressing into realm of fiction. In fact, it was poets and writers on the periphery of Buddhist studies, not the scholars in the field of history that actually undertook the task of introducing the historical Buddha in the modern Europe. Their works played an incomparably significant role in spreading the understanding of Buddhism among the masses, but the substance of the works was a reflection of their ideals of their time under the façade of the Buddha.[16]

This is as well the case with contemporary Japan. The characteristics of the historical Buddha are depicted in Japan as rational, reasonable, humane, sometimes philosophical, and even scientific, for most of these views are not the results of a critical investigation of what is to be written in historical materials, but more or less a reflection of the writers' ideals upon the image of the Buddha. They could be called as the new legends of the Buddha created by the current authors of Buddhism.

4 Documents and Works: Reconsidering Contextualism

In the history of studies on the Buddha, scholars seem to have been strongly determined that they should put the foremost priority to reconstructing a historical image of the Buddha from the existing materials. However, this is a peculiar notion. What is in need for reconsideration in fact is this attitude in dealing with the topic of the Buddha. In an effort to pursue the historical Buddha, scholars have restricted, or even transformed, both the Buddha described in texts and the texts that describe the Buddha; as a result, they cut themselves off from many other possible avenues for further research. Although the disadvantage that this attitude engenders in Buddhist studies has been paid little attention, it actually affects the understanding of the question of what Buddhism is all about.

How, then, should a text that deals with the Buddha be transformed? If readers take up a text on the Buddha with the single aim of extracting the historical Buddha, the reason d'être of the text is restricted to something that gives to them indices about the Buddha only from the viewpoint of something "historical." Even if the text contains lots of other important information, or if it is filled with rich and complex content that does not allow an easy interpretation of the Buddha therein, they end up being neglected. What comes from this attempt of reading is a text well understandable only from the viewpoint of the historicity of the

Buddha. This, however, does not mean that the text is being read but that the text is being reduced to something simple enough for the readers to avoid reading the contents they find too complicated.

What about the Buddha that is confined to the viewpoint of historicity? Given the pre-determined task of depicting the historical Buddha, or simply put, a "person," the question of what the Buddha is, never actually surfaces. Therefore, even if a text does describe the Buddha as an incomprehensible figure, the conflict of how to understand the Buddha in the text need not exist here, and the discourse about him in the text ends up being rejected as simply incomprehensible. This omission is to be authorized because it has been agreed at the beginning of the study that the Buddha that is unsuitable for the framework of a historical figure is no longer the Buddha. In the process of seeking the historical Buddha, the significance of the Buddha is not revealed as a whole but portrayed only based on a small piece of information, with a huge amount of the rest of information completely abandoned.

Thus considered, the moment scholars embrace the aim of extracting the historical Buddha from Buddhist scriptures, conditions have been set for the researchers such that they need not to read the texts or study the Buddha in the strict sense of the word. Consequently, both the effort to read and understand Buddhist scriptures and to elucidate the idea of the Buddha becomes insubstantial. This is too important an issue to overlook in terms of textual research, where the research, assumed to have been making remarkable progress, has in fact made the reading of Buddhist texts and the discussions on the theme poor and fragile.

This problem, however, seems to go beyond the realm of Buddhist studies, not to mention the study of the historical Buddha, but lead to an issue to be shared generally in the science of history. Hayden White, an American critic in the field of history, once said, "In and after the nineteenth century, history has gradually become a shelter for all the 'sane' people who are great at finding the simple among things so complex, and the familiar among things so foreign." His remark exhibits that the real problem lies in the very attitude of historical studies toward texts transmitted from the past.[17]

Buddhist scholars have taken it for granted to read a text in the context of history, as if that is to be the ultimate method of reading a text. The main focus of representative works on Buddhism, such as *Theravāda Buddhism* by Richard Gombrich, to say nothing of the *Gotama Buddha* by Nakamura Hajime, is usually placed on revealing the social, cultural, or religious context surrounding the Buddha on which backdrop to picture the historical figure. This method of reading Buddhist scriptures has become so predominant that there is no room left for its critique.

The historical studies of the twentieth century, however, have undergone a lot of soul-searching, more deeply than any previous period of time, on the general issue of how to face and deal with texts from the past. In order to review the significance of studies of the Buddha in terms of this new reflection of history, it would be helpful to refer to the discussions by Dominick LaCapra that discusses and studies on the history of thought. LaCapra reviews a text from the two different perspectives, that of its "documentary aspect" and of the "work-like aspect."

According to his understanding, when a reader deals with a text as a 'document' of historical sources, he or she unilaterally recreates the historical context of the text, and at this time, it is only the text that is subjected to change. When a reader reads a text as a 'work,' however, a dialogue arises between the reader in the present and the work from the past and, on this occasion, not only the text but also the reader will go through transformations as he or she reads along with the text. The more the texts from the past are worthy of qualifying as 'classical,' the more likely it is that they will have the power to resist the conventional presumption, to draw readers into serious emotional or intellectual conflict, and will eventually change the readers' world-view as well as their self-awareness.

Since the 'work-like aspect' argued by LaCapra concerns the topic of how readers should grapple with past texts,, this aspect seems to be, indeed, suggestive in elucidating the process of how Buddhist scriptures were produced in ancient India. Buddhist sutras, seen historically, have functioned more as 'works' than as 'documents,' and have been inherited and created through dialogues between the 'author (compiler)' of texts and their readers. To properly understand the texts endowed with these characteristics, we need to pay much attention to the process by which they are changed through dialogue.[18]

These characteristics of classical texts are exactly those of the Buddhist texts in the world of Buddhism; especially, the texts describing the Buddha have functioned as 'works' rather than as 'documents.' Steven Collins' studies on 'nirvāṇa' and John Strong's recent studies on the stories of the Buddha have endeavored to propose rereading as 'works,' the Buddhist texts that have been routinely regarded merely as historical documents.[19]

When reading a past text, listing up the elements particular to the text in a particular past and unilaterally reducing the text to these elements — in other words, confining the text within the historical context in the general sense of the word — is not the only method of reading. Along with these activities, it must be taken into consideration that a dialogue will be invoked between the past and the present, which will transform the present of the reader; especially, in the case of classical texts, which produce new interpretations of them every time they are read, every new reader can find things no one else has noticed before, creating new interpretations. This process is an approach to texts, often referred to as hermeneutics, and is an indispensable activity in the Buddhist textual studies.

5 Hagiographies as Mirrors

The scriptures dealing with the Buddha as their focal issue seem to be the most appropriate for discussing as the topic of something 'work-like.' Describing the Buddha, at least for Buddhist followers, is far from the simple activity of making objective records of a particular individual; instead, one of the main purposes of the stories of the Buddha that provide an encounter with the Buddha in narratives is to share the meaning of this encounter among those in deferent generations. Noteworthy in doing this activity is that both the writers and the readers of these stories will keep trying to answer the question of what the Buddha and his teachings are, and that their efforts will cause inner changes in the readers that they have never before experienced.

This function attested in the stories of the Buddha can be regarded as similar to that inherited in a specific genre of text categorized as hagiography. As well-known studies by Stanley Tambiah and Reginald Ray have pointed out, what people in the past have witnessed in saints is the manifestation of the ultimate value of the religion the saints represented.[20] Hagiographies serve as role models, which the followers of the saints use to adore their attitudes, to be synthetic with their lives, and to go along the same path that the saints did in their lives. If the saints' biographies are passed down beyond the boundaries of times, of areas, and of cultures, they, getting liberated from the restrictions of historical context, can create dialogues between the past and the present, and can cause changes that will connect past discoveries with current changes. One of the examples of this is the description of Sākyamuni in 'the stories of the Buddha,' covering the time when he left home to be a Buddhist priest until his death. His way of life through this period has served as an ideal for the Buddhists to follow him and as a mirror on which they reflect their own way of life.

This point is well-summarized in John Hooley's work on "saints," wherein he examines the characteristics of the Buddha seen in the narratives.[21] Hooley divides all the attributes of a saint into three elements: "examples," "fellowship," and "aid." The concept of "examples" contains significant ambiguity and precedes the other two elements. The way in which a saint lives is no doubt a simple example for his followers to learn much from their everyday life, but, at the same time, the saint's life must have absoluteness that can serve as a perpetual, eternal mirror for the followers in their ever-changing historical situations. That is, while the example represents an ideal manifestation of a religion that exists within the reach of the followers, the example also has to be an ideal, far ahead of them, too difficult to reach. When the followers of a saint trace the path of the saint, he provides "fellowship" with them by getting himself involved in them and being with them. When they feel helpless on the way, the saints, descending from the absolute world, for example, of nirvāṇa, becomes an aid for them, offering them a warm, helping hand.

This image of the saint depicted by Hooley precisely matches those of the Buddha and bodhisattvas that appear in many of the stories of the Buddha. According to these stories, the Buddha and bodhisattvas normally lead their lives as others do, while, on the other side, the Buddha and bodhisattvas sometimes display distinctive actions and attributes that ordinary people cannot imitate at all. This is exactly consonant with the ambiguity peculiar to the saints. The episode of a poor grass cutter making an offering of what little straw he has to the Buddha for him to sit on can be categorized as an example of the former, while numerous episodes of self-sacrifice by King Civi beyond the reach of imagination have to be included among the examples of the latter. The episode of the action of the bodhisattva Sumedha laying his hair over the mud so that the Buddha Dipaṃkara could walk on it — the episode seen as the very origin among all the bodhisattva trainings of being self-giving to the Buddha — seems to be located at the crossing point of these two types.

In any case, the ambiguity of bodhisattvas, in which they exist extremely close to ordinary people as fellows, while they sometimes become object of worship due to their distinctively sublime attributes, is a characteristic inherited by the saints who have achieved what seems impossible to ordinary people, that is, to realize the ultimate value in this world. The Buddha can be seen as an ultimate form of the completed actions that various saints in the state of bodhisattva should perform. The appearance of the Buddha exhibits both familiarity and an aura of grandeur. The Buddha who receives the smallest gift as an offering, and the Buddha who is equipped with thirty-two distinctively magnificent physical features towering over the public are both indispensable to the entity that is revealed as the ideal of Buddhism.

6 The Buddha in Narratives: History and Buddhism Being Generated

To reiterate a main point of this paper: the attempt to confine studies on the Buddha in historical context leads readers to a trivializing situation both of the significance of a text and that of the Buddha. The revelation of the historical restrictions of a certain world in the past could do nothing but to pinpoint the conditions that cannot apply to the current world. Once this task is completed, the 'work-like' aspect of the text will be erased and the function of the text that can change the present of the reader will disappear.

The Buddha confirmed in the form of narratives, however, is provided with the characteristics of examples, fellowship, and aid; and the stories of the Buddha are equipped with a universal structure as the stories of saints, which would go beyond the particular restrictions of a world of India in the past. The Buddha discussed in these stories is not as a historical figure in the past, but as a saint who appears at any time in the contemporary world.

If the stories of the Buddha exceed historical restrictions, it seems that they transform and recreate themselves as time goes by. John Strong's latest masterpiece, *The Relics of the Buddha*, analyzes in great detail the characteristics and functions of the Buddha's relics in the world of Buddhism as typified by stūpas that have spread throughout Southeast Asia since the time of ancient India. As this work shows, the 'stories concerning the Buddha,' which continue to regenerate themselves in a history that keeps regenerating itself, are the convincing demonstrations of the 'work-like' functions of the reality-changing characteristic inherent in the stories of the Buddha. The footsteps of the Buddha had to be traced not only within the Indian subcontinent, but also in Sri Lanka, Thailand, and all the way to Myanmar. This is the 'historical reality' concerning the dissemination of 'the Buddha.'[22]

The argument above, however, should sound quite natural if the word 'history' is reconsidered in its deeper sense. 'Being historical' means, among other things, the state of being transformed and generated. In fact, when 'the Dharma' is being dealt with as the developments and changes of thoughts in Buddhism, and the Saṃgha as the process of the formations and transformations of Buddhist communities, these two treasures are captured exactly from their historical standpoints. If so, there has to be an attempt to capture 'the Buddha' from the same historical standpoint as the other two, and redefine 'the Buddha' as something that changes and develops in the course of history as well. As mentioned, the regeneration of 'the Buddha' in a particular world in history as suitable to its particular time has taken place recurrently in the real Buddhist world. It is this fact that the Buddhist scholars should have to deal with as the object of their study. If Buddhist studies are to position themselves as one of the sciences of history in their deeper sense, Buddhist scholars will have to redefine the significance of history in cooperation with scholars of historical studies to find the 'the historical Buddha in the sense that he exists with history.'

Notes

1 This paper follows other papers of mine: M. Shimoda, "What is Buddha? The Collection of Academic Papers on Buddhism," *Journal of Komazawa Junior College*, 5, 1999, pp. 1-17; "Reconsiderations of the Concept of 'Deification of Buddha,' "*Religious Studies*, 319, 1999, pp. 217-272; "Buddha and Truth: Rethinking the 'Deification of Buddha,' "*Buddha: His Long Journey*, Volume 1, Location: NHK Publishing, 1998, pp. 169-174. Also refer to: M. Shimoda, "Reconsidering the Concept of Buddha: Focusing on the Methodology in Modern Buddhist Studies," The 5th Japan-Indian Symposium (unpublished), 1999; "Liberating Ourselves from Modernity," Annual Conference of American Academy of Religion, (unpublished), 2003.

2 Cf. H. Nakamura (Trans. by G. Sekimori), Gotama Buddha: A Biography Based on the Most Reliable Texts, Vol.1 2000, Vol.2, 2005, Tokyo: Kosei Publising Co.

This issue is briefly discussed in the following papers: M. Shimoda, *A Study of the Mahāparinirvāṇasūtra: With a Focus on the Methodology of the Mahayanasutras*, Tokyo: Shunjusha, 1997, pp. 20-22, 469-427. Refer to de Jong's *The History of Buddhist Studies*, translated by Akira Hirakawa, Tokyo: Shunjusha, 1975. It would be useful to refer to the summary in which de Jong quotes Alfred Fouche as saying, "Senart's Buddha lacks in the real human, and Ordenberg's Buddha lacks in a god,"adding, "it will be possible to decide the exact positions of the future scholars by positioning Senart and Kern on one side of the spectrum, by placing Ordenberg on its other side, or in relationship with Senart or Ordenberg." (*The History of Buddhist Studies*, p. 37) Also refer to Shimoda's *A Study*, pp. 471–472.

4 As for this issue, refer to M. Shimoda, "Buddhist studies and the Spirit of the Times,"*Ryukokushidan*, 122, pp. 27-55, 2005; "Modern Buddhist Studies and Buddhism,"*Bukkyogaku Semina*, 73, 2001, pp. 97-118.

5 P. Bigandet, *The Life of or Legend of Gaudama: The Budha of Burmese*, Rangoon, 1859; Ph. FoucauFoucaux, *Rgya tcher rol pa: Histoire du Bouddha Sakya Mouni traduite du tibétain*, Paris, 1860; do. *Le Lalita Vistara: Development des jeux*, Paris, 1884; V. Fausbøll, *The Jataka Together with Its Commentary: Being Tales of the Anterior Births of Gotama Buddha,* 6 vols., London:, 1877; T.W. Rhys Davids, *Buddhist Birth Stories of Jataka Tales*, London:, 1880; Samuel Beal, *The Romantic Legend of Sakya Buddha*, 1875; Léon Feer, *A vadāna-çataka: Cent Légendes (bouddhiques)*, Paris, 1891; James Gray, *Jinālaṃkāra or "Embellishments of Buddha by Buddharakkhita,"* London, 1894.

6 Emile Sénart, *Essai sur le légende bu Bouddha*, Paris, 1882.

7 Hendrik Kern, *Manual of Indian Buddhism*, Strasbourg, 1884; Herman Oldernberg, *Buddha, sein Leben, seine Lehre, seine Gemeinde*, Berlin, 1881; T.W. Rhys Davids, "Buddhism,"*The Encyclopedia Britannica*, IV, pp. 424-438, 1876, *Buddhism*, 1887, Edward Thomas, *The Life of the Buddha as Legend and History,* London, 1927; Alfred Foucher, *La vie du Bouddha*, Paris, 1949.In addition, Max Müller was interested in analysis of the whole myths and religions beyond the framework of

the studies of Christianity. He also took an interest in Buddhism as a form of a religion with a universal character, and did not try to reduce religious texts to historical entities. All his interests resulted in the completion of his landmark work, *Sacred Books of the East.* In the process of compiling these volumes, he pinpointed five Eastern regions, namely, India, Persia, China, Palestine, and Arabia, as the birthplaces of canonical scriptures, and strived to find a field of studies comprehensible as a religion for the West for the first time which went beyond the limitations of Christianity. Müller considered myths and canonical scriptures as two opposite, but closely related, entities that developed based on language, and thought it would be absolutely necessary to decipher their metaphors to understand their whole pictures. In this respect, it is fair to say that the issues brought up in this paper were already pointed out by Müller on a much larger scale. Hiroshi Tsuchiya's *Religions that Became Sutras* (Sapporo Hokkaido University Publishing, 2002) presents useful arguments on this theme.

8 See P. Ricoeur, *Temps et récit*, tome 1-3, Paris, 1983-1985.

9 E. J. Thomas, *op. cit.*, pp. xvii-xviii.

10 The method Buddhist scholars have conventionally adopted for reaching the oldest layer of given texts that regards the common elements attested in different materials belonging to different lineages is extremely problematic. This theme is discussed in M. Shimoda (1997 p. 26-27, see note 3). G. Schopen, "Two Problems in the History of Buddhism: The Layman/ Monk Distinction and the Doctrine of the Transference of Merits,"*Studien zur Indologie und Iranistik*, 10, pp. 9-47, 1985 (Cf. G. Schopen, *Bones, Stones and Buddhist Monks: Collected Papers on the Archaeology, Epigraphy and Texts of Monastic Buddhism in India*, Hololulu, 1997) and R. F. Gombrich, "Recovering the Buddha's Message," D. Seyfort Ruegg and L. Schimithausen (eds.) *Earliest Buddhism and Madhyamika,* Vol. 2, London, pp.1-23, 1990.

11 R.S. Copleston, *The Quarterly Review,* 1890, p. 327.

12 R. Armstrong, "Buddhism and Christianity,"*The Theological Review*, 7, 1870, pp. 176-200 (esp. p. 199).

13 Ch. Speir, *Life in Ancient India,* London, 1856, p. 288; Agnes M. Machar, "Buddha and Buddhism," p. 35, *Religious Systems of the World,* London, 1890; T.W. Rhys Davids, "Buddha's First Sermon," *Fortnightly Review*, 32, 1879 (pp. 899-911) p. 901.

14 S. Collins, *Selfless Persons: Imagery and Thought in Theravada Buddhism*, Cambridge: Cambridge University Press, 1982, introduction. In addition, as for differences between the discourse by the Buddha and the description about the Buddha, refer to Yamada Ryujo's *Daijo bukkyo kenkyu josetsu* (*Introduction to the Theory of the Establishment of Mahayana Buddhism*) Kyoto: Heirakuji Books, 1959, p. 138. Robinson's following argument also overlaps with that of this paper, especially the one in Chapter 5: "The quest for the objective Gautama ... is foredoomed to a measure of failure. We cannot get behind the portrait that the early communities synthesized for their founders; their reports are all we have. But though the Community (Sangha) created the image of the Buddha, the Buddha created the Community and in so doing impressed upon it his personality. The master exhorted his disciples to imitate him, and they formulated and transmitted an image of him, along with his teachings, as a model for later generations to imitate." (R.H. Robinson, *The Buddhist Religion*, Enrico, 1970, p. 13.)

15 Refer to M. Shimoda's following three papers: "Hotoke towa nanika (What Is the Buddha),"*The Collection of Academic Papers on Buddhism*, Komazawa Junior College, #5, 1999, pp. 1-17, and "Notes on the Studies of Canonical Scriptures of Indian Buddhism From the Viewpoint of Oral Transmission,"*Indotetsugaku Bukkyogaku* (*Indian Philosophy Buddhist Studies*), #17, 2002.

16 Phillip Almond, *The British Discovery of Buddhism*, Cambridge University Press, 1988; Roger-Pol Droi, *Le culte du néant: Les philosophes et le bouddha*, Paris: Seul, 1997. Also refer to *Buddhist Studies and the Spirit of the Times*, *Rykokushidan*, #122. As for Almond's arguments, the following excellent review will be of help: J. Silk, "The Victorian Creation of Buddhism," *Journal of Indian Philosophy*, 22, pp. 171-196, 1994.

17 Hayden White, *Tropics of Discourse*, Baltimore: The John Hopkins University Press, 1978, p. 30.

18 Dominick LaCapra, *Rethinking Intellectual History:Texts, Contents, Language*, Cornell University Press, 1983. LaCapra says that he owes his idea of "work-like" to the arguments in the following book: Martin Heidegger, *Der Ursprung des Kunstwerkes*, Stuttgart, 1960. He also states that distinctions between "documentary" and "work-like" can be compared to the relationship between "contestitive" and "performative,"proposed by John Austin. The former refers to descriptive statements judged by the criteria of right or wrong depending on how to respond to facts, while the latter conducts activities that bring changes to circumstances through the use of words. Refer toJ. L. Austin, *How to Do Things with Words*, Harvard University Press, 1955, (2nd ed. 1975, Harvard University Press).

19 S. Collins, *Nirvana and Other Buddhist Felicities: Utopias of the Pali Imaginaire*, Cambridge University Press, 1997; J. Strong, *The Buddha: A Short Biography*, Oxford, 2001.

20 S. Thambiah, *The Buddhist Saints of the Forest and the Cult of Amulets: A Study in Charisma, Hagiography, Sectarianism, and Millennial Buddhism*, Cambridge University Press, 1984, pp. 111-123; R. Ray *Buddhist Saints in India: A Study in Buddhist Values and Orientations*, Oxford University Press, 1994. These two researches are no doubt useful, but they do not particularly develop arguments concerning "saints" as this paper does.

21 J. S. Hawley (ed.), *Saints and Virtues*, University of California Press, 1987.

22 J. Strong, *Relics of the Buddha,* Princeton University Press, 2004.

Dancing Gaṇeśa*

–in India and beyond its Frontiers–

Sudha Malaiya

Dance has always constituted the life breath of the culture of the world and especially in India, where not only mortal human beings but also immortal gods dance. There is a galaxy of major gods and goddesses of the Hindu pantheon who dance. The distinguished among them is the elephant-headed, Gaṇeśa, the son of Śiva.

The mythology surrounding the origin and development of the iconography of Gaṇeśa, as a deity to be worshipped, is a complete mystery to the academic world. There are frequent references in the early literature to Gaṇapati as a creator of obstacles – *vighneśa* - and later as the remover of obstacles – *Vighnavināśaka*. The references about Gaṇeśa can be traced back to different textual sources of scholarly works such as: *Baudhāyana-Dharmasūtra*, *Yājñavalkya* and *Mānava-Gṛhasūtra*. However, without getting involved into the deep-rooted controversy over the question of the origin, the elephant head and the single tusk, the derivation of name etc; it may be stated that his identity, as an independent deity for worship was established at the time of the Guptas. He has frequently been mentioned in the texts called *Matsya-Purāṇa* and *Varāha-Purāṇa*, and in creative literatures such as *Kādambarī* and *Mālatīmādhava*.[1]

It is well known that Gaṇeśa achieved a very exalted position in the hierarchy of worshipping gods in a very short period. The general opinion is that the worship of him as an independent deity began in the 6th Century A.D. Furthermore, an independent sect of his followers known as *Gāṇapatya* had existed in the 10th Century; at the same time, the deity Gaṇeśa had been adopted by other religious systems such as Buddhism. Contextually, the recognition of him as a deity spread almost other parts of Asia where Buddhism and some sects of Hinduism assumed the position of prevailing faiths. The name of Gaṇeśa spread to more distant lands across Asia. In the South East Asia he was worshipped as a Hindu deity whereas in East Asia as a Buddhist deity.

A study on different kinds of arts and cultures of India needs a complete reference to the salient features of its important spread with the religion of India to other countries across Asia. The famous Sanskrit inscriptions from Cambodia, Java and Bali have reference to the Kâvya literature. The popular stories of Mahābhārata and Rāmāyaṇa are favorite themes in Javanees literature, dance, drama and music; the names of early rulers of Java, Thailand and Cambodia are all influenced by Indian names. Some aspects of Indian tradition are surviving in those countries, which have disappeared from India centuries ago. For example, in the harp of Burma, there is an element of Indian classical Indian musical instrument vīṇā. In the paleography of the early inscriptions in those countries, it is possible to find the influence of Shankarācārya who integrated various religious sects in Indian main land to places as far as Funan, in the Mekong delta.

Gaṇeśa's impressive figure influenced the culture of the Eastern countries. In spite of his deviant looks, he was accepted as an important deity. In the Mythology, he is figured as the stout dwarf goblin, the imp of Maras, Yakṣas or Gaṇas. He was even given the rank of the chieftain of gaṇas: Gaṇeśa, the 'Lord of Gaṇas'. Besides, he is associated with the dance through Śiva (Naṭarāja), the 'Lord of Dancers,' mythologically considered as Gaṇeśa's father.

Unlike Śiva who is the creator and the main authority of dance, Gaṇeśa's association with dance is uncertain and obscure. While there are numerous references to the dance of Śiva in mythology, there is no such references to Gaṇeśa. Also there are no legends, which say that Gaṇeśa actually dances. Yet his dance has been fancifully described in literature and epigraphic records and picturesquely portrayed in art. It has been universally accepted that *abhaṅgī, tribhaṅgī* and *atibhaṅgı* dance movements and postures look more attractive compared to other simpler standing postures. Furthermore, there is another reason for Vināyaka to be connected with dance. Gaṇeśa's dance is accepted as inherited from Śiva and Pārvati the greatest exponents of *tāṇḍava* and *lāsya*. This could be one aspect and as the head of the dancing of the *gaṇas* as *Bhūteśa*, could be another. The genesis of Gaṇeśa's dance can be traced to Mahābhārata, where among others, elephant-headed dancing *gaṇa* is mentioned.[2]

Gaṇeśa's relation with dance may also be traced to his obscure origins. It is believed by many that he was worshipped by village people as the village god-Asfribaladie. The god was to be pacified and propitiated first. Traditionally, this god head was connected with harvest ceremonies as the "Lord of the Harvest." As shown from the evidences, rites, ceremonies and deities associated with harvest festivals, were having many dances expressing symbolic meaning to the rituals. It could be possible that Gaṇeśa in his dancing form became a part of the ritual dancing. The elephant head, suggesting his origin, can be traced back to the old superstitious totem (an animal, plant, or object that has religious or spiritual importance for a particular group of people) worships and agrarian rites. The elephant holds a large place in Indian folklore through its large size, unequalled strength, incredible docility and surprising intelligence. Alice Getty is of the opinion that the single tusk of Gaṇeśa symbolically stands for the most important implement of the harvest, the plough. Furthermore, the word *ekandant* may be translated as the *gaṇas* who also could dance, indicating his association with dance.

In the literary texts and the southern Śaiva literature the symbolic, spiritual and aesthetic significance given to the dance of Gaṇeśa is equal to Śiva's dance. Nṛtta Gaṇapati either represents the cosmic dance of Śiva, the supreme and indivisible one or the dance of *gaṇas* who are said to be the representations of bhūtas and bhūtānshas or tattva and tattvāṁshas. It is worth mentioning that the name Gaṇeśa in the Mahābhārata is related to 'Śiva' ;and 'Gaṇapati' found in Ṛgveda to Brahmaṇaspati (Father of Gods).[3] It could be for this reason that any independent dancing episodes related to Gaṇeśa. It is to be noted that some scholars consider Śiva and Gaṇeśa to be originally one and the same. Although Gaṇeśa does not figure in the Mahābhārata as distinct from Śiva, yet he is an aspect of Śiva and might therefore, have been considered identical to the Rudra Śiva; whereas, he was introduced into the Indian pantheon as Gaṇeśa, the 'Lord of the Gaṇas'. In Yājñavalkya Samhita, the group 4 Vināyakas, addressed as one god and the son of Ambikā. According to Alice Getty, this may be considered as the earliest form of Gaṇapati. The name Vinyaka, means to create difficulties and obstacles if not properly propitiated. Mahābhārata lists 9 classes of benevolent deities as *gaṇas* who are to be called Gaṇeśa; highlighting the symbolic significance. Someshvara and Vāsukapla have graphically described it in Kathāsaritsāgara. And in Subhāṣita-Ratnakośa,[4] Gaṇeshvara`s dance in which, by showing the mirror to Śiva, he meticulously follows Śiva. Dancing in the twilight while raising his trunk in rhythmic and measured fashion, the 'Victor of obstacles' threatens and swallows the obstacles to eliminate them and thus assures *tāla* and *laya*.[5] Vāsukalpa says in *Subhāṣitaratnakośa* that his delightful dance is imitated by the elephants of the quarters who spring up as the earth trembles from the stamping of his feet.[6] Vāsukalpa also draws a parallel of *ardhanārīshvara* in Śankarā's (Śiva) son which brings him closer to his father. The single tusk or Ekadanta provides him with a hermaphrodite form, that is, represents the masculine, whereas the missing tusk symbolizes the feminine form. So Gaṇeṣa is an exponent of both the forms. He assumes this guise in his anxiety to imitate his parents Gaurī (Parvati) and Girīśa (Śiva).[7] In a beautiful picture of dancing Gaṇeśa represents his vermilion stained trunk is raised up (*uddandītaḥ karaḥ*) like a coral handle for the moon. This is close to the *ūrdhvatāṇḍava* of Shiva where Gaṇeśa has thrown his legs up as *daṇḍapāda*.[8]

The praises of the dance of the Naṭarāja's son, Gaṇeśa, have also been sung in the inscriptions. In the fourth verse of the Koni inscription of Prithvideva II of Ratanpur,[9] the post invokes blessings of *Vighnavināśaka-* the son of two mothers or *dvaimātrra* who destroys obstacles by the humming of bees intoxicated from drinking the sweet juice that gushes forth with force at the commencement of his dance. Another beautiful picture of the dancing *pārvatīnandana* is given in the Ratanpur stone inscription of Prithvideva II[10] (Year 1207). In this representation, the large forehead of his frontal globes (the *kumbhasthala* of *Vighneśvara*) are stained with brilliant vermilion and the *ugratāṇḍava* of his trunk colors the pavilion of the sky.

According to the Âgamas, the image of *nṛtta-Gaṇapati* should have eight hands and one head. However, there are other examples of four, six, eight, ten, twelve, sixteen and eighteen-handed figures with two, three, four or five heads are not rare. In Mumbai (Maharashtra), a two-headed image is worshipped at the local festivals called Gaṇeśa-Jayantī.[11] Gaṇeśa with three or four heads[12] (Japan and Indo China) and over five heads[13] (Nepal) are found only outside India. He is ornamented with *sarpayaĩnopavīta* (overhead snake), *keyūra*, *kaṅkaṇa*, *karaṇḍamukūta*, *prabhāmaṇḍala* and *ekamuktāvalīhāra*, with arms carrying his usual attributes such as axe, modaka,[14] *kuṭhāra*, *jambu* (woo apple), *radish*, styles, a bowl of cakes, *śūla* (trident), *aṅkuśa* (gourd), book, sword, pot, snake and one tusk. The radish found in Nepal, Tibet and Japan might be the misinterpretation of the tusk.[15] It is noteworthy that in Bengal Gaṇeśa is known as the one with ears like fans and teeth like radishes. Pomegranates,[16] emblems of fertility and *cintāmaṇi*[17] are also found in esoteric forms in Nepal and Tibet. Sometimes instead of *yajnopavīta* Ganesha wears a snake girdle. Together with such iconographic details of the *nṛtta* Gaṇapati images have been analyzed in terms of the vocabulary of dance as in the Nāṭyaśāstra.[18] The latter not only played a dominant role in the realm of theatre but also exercised an indispensable influence on the other arts of India.

The evolution in the image of Gaṇeśa can be traced through the form of *Gajānana-yakiśamūrti*. The elephant-headed image on the railings of Amarāvatī is considered as the prototype of Gaṇeśa by the scholars, [19] though with reservation by some others. It can be said with certainty that without a transitional stage, such as the one found in Amarāvatī, it is difficult to conceive the completed form of Gaṇeśa. The elephant-headed divinities of lesser rank were known in South and North India, Indo-China and Chinese Turkistan, but without Gaṇeśa's attributions.[20] By the time of the Guptas, the iconography of Gaṇeśa was fully developed; and independent images were also found at Mathura,[21] Bhumra[22] and Udaigiṛi. The earliest representation of the dance of Gaṇeśa had started to appear only in the Gupta and it multiplied in the medieval period.

Out of the three Gaṇeśa images mentioned by Getty, the dancing Gaṇeśa image No. 1064, preserved at Mathura Museum, is the earliest example of its kind. The two-armed elephant headed *gaṇa* like dancing figure from Bhumra might as well be taken as the *nṛtta*-Gaṇapati. Yet, the possibility of it merely as a *gaṇa* cannot be ruled out. The most important early example of dancing Gaṇeśa is from the Rājīvalochana temple, Rājim. It has an eight-armed *nṛtta*-Gaṇapati with its fully developed iconography and implements. At Bādamī[23] and Aihole he is depicted in a smaller size. He is standing slightly in a dancing pose while giving attendance to the dancing Śiva. He has his feet in *sama-traśra,* which is very near both *vaiṣṇavasthānaka*[24] and the initial position of so many *karaṇas*. In few examples he is quite close to *kaiṭisama-karaṇa*[25] where he is shown with one hand on *udvahita kati.*[26] Many Naṭarāja and *gaṇa* figures are also shown in the same pose.

An image from Hinglajgarh is a characteristic example for a number of images, in which one foot is in *kiñchita* and other in *samapāda* (normal foot position). In this four-armed *Paramāra* the *aṅguliprṣṭhaga* foot is kept on the back toe which is still a characteristic feature of contemporary dancing sculptures in India. The presence of third eye is significant which do not occur that frequently in the images of Śiva.

A similar image of Highlajgarh, Gaṇeśa is seen in *paṇavavādika* to his right. The right hand is held in *allapallava*[28] near the shoulder and the left is kept on the *kaṭI* (hip). The presence of Maheśvari and Sarasvati in the upper *parikara* is peculiar *paramāra* characteristics. At the Indore Museum, there is a rare image of dancing Gaṇeśa which is in the upper *parikara* flanked by Maheshvari and Saraswatī on each of the sides. Similar compositions can be seen among the contemporary Chandela. The Khajuraho figure of Gaṇeśa is an example that can be found in the Kandariya Mahadeo temple, with a difference that the right hand is held on the right knee in *kaṭakāmukha*.[29] The *mārdaṅgika* on the left and the snake in the left hand are noteworthy to mention. The Chandela and Kalachuri parallels from Bhandakapur and Damoh are not different from these figures.

One of the outstanding examples is the dancing Vināyaka figure in a *gaṇeśapaṭṭa* of the 9 Vināyakas now preserved at the Vikram Museum, Ujjain. Its exact identification remains to be done. They could be the same 9 class of benevolent deities, mentioned in the Mahābhārata to be called as Gaṇeśa's figure. Other examples are of the eight-armed *nṛtta*-Gaṇapati which portray the typical dance pose of this period are from Malhar and Ujjain. In the former, we see *lalita karaṇa*[30] with right *vivartita* and left *kriṣasta* and a *kuṭṭita pāda*. Occurring very frequently throughout India from the 5th to the 13th century A.D; this pose is being represented by *Naṭarājas* and *gaṇas* as well. Except for the difference in the conventional attributes of Gaṇeśa, Naṭarājas and *gaṇas*, the treatment of the body in these images is just the same. The

Gajavaktra from Ujjain depicted with one leg lifted and the knee facing sideways represents the *pārśvajānu karaṇa*;[31] holding the ears like Śiva, this figure holds the snake over the head. Moreover, the eight-armed Gaṇapati from Highlajgarh can also be seen representing *ūrdhvajānu*[32] with the overhead snake and one tusk in the right hand. This reminds us of the tempestuous *tāṇḍava* of Gaṇapati trampling the earth by his tread as fancied by the poet Vāsukalpa. The *ūrdhvajānu* is also ideally represented by the *gaṇas* and Naṭarājas of Central India. There are examples of a clear *daṇḍpakṣa karaṇa* with the knee facing upwards in *ūrdhvajānu* and one arm with an extended staff like in *daṇḍapakṣa hasta*.[34]

While there are many representation scenes of Śiva dancing in the company of goddesses acting as accompanists, there are few such examples of dancing Gaṇeśa where he dances with other accompanists represented in the same size. The four-armed Gaapati from Sagar District, dancing in the company of a female flutist and a drummer, is one of its kinds. In contrast, the examples of Gaapati dancing amidst *Vīrabhadra* and *saptamātṛkās* who are the feminine counterparts of the seven great Brāhmaṇa gods created in *Andhakāsura* battle, are many and found at various places. The large panel preserved in the Allahabad museum from Gurgi,[35] is a masterpiece sculpture. Also worthy of mentioning is the example that is found in the caving at "the *shiradala* of *toraṇa-Mandira* at Gyaraspur." This is unique in many respects. *Gaṇa* is seen here in a pose representing the well known Śiva image in bronze. This pose, which has been placed at Bhumra predates its southern counterparts.

Though it had vanished altogether at the time of the Gupta period, it became immensely popular in South India. We have not yet come across any further examples of either Naṭarāja or *gaṇa* or Gaṇapati in a late period other than these images. The pose has not been represented even in any other dance sculpture, except the one from Lakṣmaṇa Temple in Khajurāho, where there is an image in a panel with a few *gaṇa* like figures. One more striking aspect of this panel is that the image of Vīrabhadra is multi-armed and he is seen dancing on a trampled human figure. This human figure could be *apasmāra*. Unfortunately, there are no other examples of *apasmāra's* presence, which is mainly a South Indian feature, in North India, the exact identification of this human figure is yet to be established and calls for further research in future.

Incidentally, the examples of *Vighnāntaka* dancing in the company of *navagṛhas* as seen in Southern and Eastern art, are conspicuously absent in North and Central India. Even though tradition says that Gaṇeśa has brought into being the drum as an accompaniment for dance.[36] A sculptural representation of Gaṇeśa playing on flute is found at Mallikārjuna temple, Sri Sailam, but in Central India no such example has so far been found except the very few examples where he is acting as an accompanist to Śiva's dance.

Also in the Gupta period, the *swastika-pāda* or cross legged position represented frequently. In the Gupta period for Naṭarāja figures is not seen either in *gaṇa* or Gaṇapati figures. Similarly the *vṛchika-pāda*[37] and *lalāṭatilaka*[38] or *ūrdhvatāṇḍava* pose so frequently depicted in the art of South India, is unrepresented in the *gaṇas* figures of North India during the Gupta period. And they are unrepresented by nṛtta-Gaṇapati and Naṭarājas images of Central India. At this time, the twisted waist and posterior views were portrayed by *Paramāra* and Chandella Naṭarājas are also significantly absent except in the above mentioned Gyaraspur example. Perhaps artists did not take the risk of depicting the pot bellied and elephant-headed god with a twisted waist.

The vehicle of Gaṇeśa is also depicted in a manner similar to Śiva, usually on the right side and at times below the *pādapīṭha*. The tradition of Śiva dancing on a bull is also shown as being imitated by Gaṇeśa. He is even depicted as dancing on a rat in an image in a small temple of Ṛehli (Sagar), *Ekadanta* has also occasionally adopted in Chandraśekhara's *ardha Chandra* on his head, justifying his name Bhālachandra. There is however, a striking dissimilarity in the vehicles of the father and the son. Śiva's Nandī takes equal delight in his Master's dance, either by himself sharing the pleasure of dancing or by faithfully watching the performance, whereas Gaṇeśa's *mūṣika* is always seen partaking of his share in the *prasāda* rather than observing his Lord's performance as a keen spectator. Furthermore *Karaṇḍa-mukuṭa* is strikingly absent in many examples of Gaṇeśa In India the example does not wear a skull head like Śiva, although in Java there are such images. Similarly the conch shell which is seen in the Indian examples from Indochina is also absent in India.

Khotan, Mangolia and Afghanistan

In Khotan, images of Gaṇeśa are found with Indian features as well as typical Chinese and Turkestan features. However, nṛta-Gaṇapati is altogether absent in any of these images. In Mongolia Hinduism reached together with Buddhism via Tibet in the 13th century. The dancing form of Gaṇeśa is even listed among the 'Five Hundred gods of Nar-than', with left foot holding down a rat, the right leg bent, and the four hands holding an axe, a radish, sweets and a trident, seldom carried by him. Nevertheless, there is no image of Gaṇeśa in a dancing attitude has been found. No images of this kind are available in 5th-and 6th centuries from Afghanistan to show Gaṇeśa in dancing attitude. However, it is interesting to note such an early representation of Gaṇeśa is found in the land of 'Ariana' which was, of course, was a part of mainland India at one time.

Nepal

The introduction of Gaṇeśa in Nepal is difficult to date but existing sculptural evidence shows that he was quite popular and was adored by both Hindus and Buddhists from the 10th century. In Buddhism he is known as *'Siddhidātā'* 'the giver of success', and even a mystic mantra, the *Gaṇapatihṛdya*[39] revealed to Ānanda by Buddha, is associated with Gaṇeśa by the Buddhist tradition. A large number of Gaṇeśa images have been found in Nepal, yet none of them is having the independent dancing Gaṇeśa sculptures. In contrast, iṅ Buddhist art of Nepal and Tibet Gaṇeśa is represented as a Hindu demon called Vināyaka, crouching under the feet of lotus throne of Buddhist Goddess Bhṛkuṭi-Tārā.[40] At the same time, as the Buddhist god Bināyaka, he should have been depicted in dancing pose but this is only seen in paintings.[41] In India nṛtta-Gaṇapati, if painted, had to be conceived in yellow with the bending right leg, the left leg raising up in *ūrdhvajānu* and 4 to 16 arms carrying the conventional attributes. In contrast, in Nepal paintings are conceived in red with the right leg holding down a rat, the left one lifted up in extreme position, 12 arms, a third eye and an ornamentel crown.[42] 10 arms of the figure of Gaṇeśa carry the usual tântrika symbols and the other two hold a radish and cintâmaṇi in contrast to the tusk and modaka seen in Indian images. He is also surrounded by four Vināyakas- *Rakta*, *Chandra*, *Siddhi* and *Aśoka*- all in dancing attitude, thus making an assembly of five deities to indicate the group of Buddhist gods whose central figure known as Sūrya Vināyaka. It is to be noted that in Nepal along with other temples of Gaṇesha[43], a Buddhist temple dedicated to five Gaṇapati is also found. Nepalese tradition trace Gaṇapati's origin not from any of the Hindu legends in which Śiva and Parvati created him, but he became visible in a sun ray, hence his name *Sūrya-Vināyaka*.

In stone or bronze Gaṇeśa is found dancing only in attendance to Śiva and Pārvatī in many images. In a number of Umā-Maheshvara images found in Nepal, he is represented as a four-armed dancing Gaṇesha in the lower tier with the gaṇas. The earliest of the typical, well presented steles[44] showing umā-Maheshvara with Gaṅgādhara aspect of Śiva in the usual setting and composition with family members and attendants, (C. 9th century) is from the *Kumbhesvaratank*, *Patan*. It shows Śiva and Pārvatī seated in the Kailâsa in *padmāsana* and *sukhāsana* respectively. Gaṅgā is shown, on the top, as descending headlong. The pedestal forming the lowest tier is the four-armed Gaṇeśa shown as dancing with *gaṇas*. The seated *Uluka-mukha* is playing flute, on the left side dancing *Kumbhāṇḍa Ghanṭākarṇa* and *Bhṛgī* are shown; *Siṁhamukha* is playing a drum and the seated *Vānaramukha* pose is playing on cymbal. Gaṇesha is dancing in the *ardhamaṇḍalī* position with both the *tryaśra* feet kept apart in *maṇḍalasthānaka*. Unfortunately the left hand is broken and it is under doubt whether the right hand is actually in *varadapatāka hasta*.

All the stele[45] from *Gairidhara, Patan*, has the *Gangadhara* aspect with the typical Nepalese faces representing Śiva and Pārvatī in *ardhaparyaṅkasāna*. In the lower tier a four-armed Gaṇeśa is dancing together with *Bhṛṅgī* and *Kumbhāṇa* on either side while other *gaṇas* are playing instruments. In another stele from *Gairidhara*, in *Patan* (12th century) Gaṇeśa is represented in the initial position of *pārśvajānu* with the uplifted leg facing sideways. The right arm is spread out like a staff to bring him closer to the *daṇḍapakṣa-karaṇa*. The other hands carry the usual attributes. Yet another example[46] of the same category from Patan has four-armed Gaṇeśa in lower tier also dancing, though on a different leg. A noteworthy feature of this depiction is Himalayan hill scope shown in conical configuration.

Ten-armed and five-headed Gaṇeśa mounted on a lion and known as '*Heramba*' is the most popular form of Gaṇeśa in Nepal. Though non-dancing, mention can be made of the two three *Heramba* images or which show a rat or rat and lion under each foot of the god and a five-hooded *nāga* over the head[47]. The pose can be identified in dance terminology with *alīḍha-sthānaka*. According to Dhavalikar, it appears to have been taken from one of the dancing forms of Śiva (Naṭarāja) and shows Gaṇeśa`s connection with Śiva. Nepalese were well acquainted with the Naṭarājas and *nṛtta-Gaṇapati* images of North India. This is also clear from the images of nṛtta-Gaṇeśa holding the overhead snake in Nepal, which are very common in India. A typical panel of Gaṇeśa dancing with seven mothers has not been discovered in Nepal but eight goddesses are represented in one scene at a temple in *Kirtipur*. The eighth is possibly looked upon as the Śakti of Gaṇeśa. The *aṣṭamātṛkā* panel does not exist in India.

Tibet

In Tibet Gaṇeśa never became popular in the pantheon of Mahāyāṇa Buddhism. But Gaṇeśa is either accorded the role of the *dvārapāla* or was degraded to the point of being trodden on by *Mahākāla*, *Aparājitā*, *Vighnāntaka* or *Mañjushrī*. Surprisingly no dancing image of Gaṇeśa has so far been discovered in Tibet.

Burma, Siam and Indo-China

Along with the trader colonists of India in Burma, Thailand (Siam) and Indo-China, (Cambodia and Vietnam) started the process of Indianization of these countries with the advent of Buddhism and the worship of Indian gods. Indeed the findings of sculptures, in the style of 'Later Andharas' in Java and Celebes indicate the spread of Indian Buddhism in all over the South-eastern Asia. The Indian influences are evident in the Pre-Khmer civilization of 5th, 6th and 7th century. Names of its kinds after natural regions of India and Śiva would reveal the close Indian contacts. Brick ornamentation of the temple of *Sambor* (Cambodia) suggests the Indian precedence of Sirpur and Bhitarīgāon. The Śiva Temple of *Bayang* (Burma) reminds us of the shrine at *Bhima's rath* at Mamallapuram. Sculptures of pre-Khmer period reveals an indebtedness to Indian models and are so closely related to Gupta sculptures that possibility of their having been carved by continuous alternation between Buddhism and Hinduism throughout the history of Cambodia.

Hinduism penetrated into Burma long before the introduction of Buddhism, which is evident from the large number of Hindu gods found in that country. The Hindu traders looking forward for success in trade carried the images of the "Remover of Obstacles" with them. Statues of Gaṇeśa have been found in lower Burma especially in the deltaic region, but none of them is of interest to this study. The region of Siam also came into contact with India at a very early period; the influence of the elements of the Amarāvatī school and then the Gupta, Pallava and pāla are noticeable in the Siamese art. The Mons was devoted Hindus. Gaṇeśa became popular with the Buddhists as well as the Brāhmins. But again no dancing images of Gaṇeśa have been found in Ayuthian (Ayodhya) art of Central Siam. The cult of Śiva penetrated into Cambodia from Funan, where Brahmanism was practiced at a very early date. There are many temples of Śiva and Gaṇeśa dedicated to them (*Prasat Bak*, 10th century temple). Unfortunately, the Khmer representations of Gaṇeśa, also known as *Praha Kenes*, contain few independent dancing images. Although dancing Gaṇeśa accompanying Śiva can be seen in the temples of *Shri Vijaya*, Benteaisrei (9th century AD), *Phnom Chisor*, and *Baset.* In a lintel[48] from *Prah Pithu* representing ten-armed Śiva dancing with Brahmā and Viṣṇu keeping time for him, depicts Gaṇeśa as one of the spectators. In fact the Cham dynasty held Śaivism in such a high esteem that its heads claimed direct descent from Śiva. Epigraphical evidences show that the temples were dedicated to Gaṇeśa and images of Gaṇeśa have been found, to indicate the popularity of the Gaṇeśa cult. The occurrence of *uṣṇīṣa*, similar to Buddha, on the Gaṇeśa's head establishes the Buddhist influence on Hindu Images. However, no dancing Gaṇeśa has been found in *Champa*. At *Ben-Mala* and *Banteai Samre*, there are other images of dancing Śiva[49] flanked by Umā and Gaṇeśa (9th century AD). Also noted scholar, Coedas has described a few dancing figures of Śiva from Angkorwat and Ben Mealea, in which Śiva (Naṭarāja) is accompanied by Gaṇeśa with other Gods and celestials.

Indonesia

Brahmanism flourished in the Malay Archepelago as early as 5th century when Fahien visited Java (*Yava-dvipa*) and reported many sanctuaries dedicated to Śiva until 8th century AD. Images of Gaṇeśa, also started appearing in large numbers. But there is no existing evidence of Gaṇeśa temples or indications of the prevalence of ancient Gaṇeśa cult. In Java, no images of interest have so far been discovered. In Indonesia, except one in Ardmelijo, near Singasari, Java, is reported by Dhaky. It depicts a triad of three deities in which Gaṇeśa is in a slightly dancing pose. He is standing to the right of the Nepalese Goddess *Guhyeshvarī* and *Chakrạchakra* to the left of her.

In Bali Gaṇeśa was worshipped amongst the group of five deities: Śiva, Durgā, Viṣṇu, Sūrya and Gaṇeśa. But there is no evidence of any independent Gaṇeśa images. Today Gaṇeśa is worshipped especially in Tjandi niches as the 'protector against evil spirit'. In another form he is invariably present to the extreme right of Balinese groups of defied personages in which form he must have been originally worshipped as the "Remover of Obstacles". Again no images of Gaṇeśa exist in Bali now.

China and Japan

Despite the earliest known image of Gaṇeśa have been reported from China, where he is referred to as the "spirit king of elephants", no nṛtta-Gaṇapati image has been found there. None of the forms of Gaṇeśa is known in China and Japan, but there is one single form is known as Vinayaka, and the other double form is called Kāngiten, but neither of them is connected with dance.

Conclusion

Notwithstanding Gaṇeśa's ungainly elephant head, cunning little eyes, and unusual expression, short arms, bulging girth, stunted legs, and huge trunk swaying from side to side, all these images convey a certain sense of dynamism and rhythm, together with humour, as the essence of the art. In India, wherever the artists used their creative genius, the results were astounding. However stereotyped mass production of the images often result in the stylization of the iconography in the imagery. This led to the lack of variety into the amount of imagination in Gaṇeśa images. As regards *nṛtta*-Gaṇapati beyond the Indian frontiers as shown in the above analysis reveals that though Gaṇeśa was equally popular in distant Lands, his dance form, except in Nepal, did not enjoy popularity as it was for Śiva. Surprisingly there is no lack of evidence of other non-secular and secular music and dance sculptures especially in Burma (*Srikṣetra* and *Pagan*), Indonesia, (*Lara-djjongrang, Prambanan, Ḅorobudur*), Thailand, Champa and Cambodia. They followed more or less a dance style, identical in principles of movement, proving thereby an active dialogue that was not copying or just influence but an interaction of form and technique, with regional distinctiveness. The stylization in sculpture and dance in India and beyond its frontier emerges from basic *ardhamaṇḍalī* position. It is thereby amazing to note the conspicuous absence of independent dancing Gaṇeśa images in these countries where Śiva's dancing form proliferates.

Notes

* This study is with special reference to Central India.

1 See, Alice Getty – Ganeṣa, Delhi 2nd ed, 1971, p. 1-9.

2 See, Sudha Malaiya, "Dancing Gaṇas in Early Art of Madhya Pradesh" Delhi, 1987, p. 177-181.

3 Ibid, p. 2-5.

4 See, C. Shivaramamurti, Naṭarāja in Art. Thought and Literature. Delhi, 1965, p. 70,71.

5 Kathasarit-sāgara of Someshvara, 27, 1.

6 Subhāṣita-ratna-kośa of Bāsukalpa, 5, 13.

7 Kathāsarit-sāgara. 105, 2 and 51, 1.

8 Subhāṣitaratnakośa, 5, 24.

9 Corpus Inscriptionum Indicarum, 4, p. 465.

10 Corpus Inscriptionum Indicarum, 4, p. 485.

11 Getty, Ibid, p. 14, Fig.1.

12 Ibid. pl. 27(c), in Indo-China, in a private collection, a small bronze image with four heads.

13 Five-headed form of Gaṇesha was most popular in Nepal with four

heads pointing to each cardinal points and fifth on top; see, Getty, ibid, p.15 &7 from Dacca also, in an example, the five heads are on the same tier i.e. two heads on the either side of the central head. See, Getty, ibid, pl. 4(b).

14 Modaka, jambu, radish, stylus and bowl of cakes are held by no other deity. Modaka is looked upon by certain sects as representing Mahā-Buddhi and others as germ of like.

15 It is never carried by Gaṇesha at the same time as the broken tusk; Getty, ibid, p. 18.

16 Goblet d'Alviella, La Migration des Symboles, p. 184.

17 Modaka is replaced by chintāmaṇi in Tibetan paintings.

18 The Nātyashastra composed by Bharata Muni is the largest and ancient available text on the art of histrionics, which deals largely with the art of theatre, dance and music put together.

19 Coomarswamy and Jouvean-Dubrevil. See, Amarāvatī, Burgess, pl. 30, no.1.

20 Getty, ibid, p. 26, is of the opinion that though earliest terracotta image of Gaṇgesha was found at the ancient site of Akra, N.W.F.P., where pre-Gupta objects as early as the second century have been discovered, yet it is not earlier than the fifth century.

21 Getty, ibid, pl. 2(a), from Sankisa Mound, Mathura.

22 Ibid, pl. 3(b).

23 See, Sivaramamurti, op.cit. p.179, fig. 17.

24 N.S., Vaisnava sthānaka.

25 N.S., Katisoma karaṇa, karaṇa is basic unit of dance compositor, composed of hand and feet movements.

26 N.S., 9.249(b).

27 Nṛtta-Ratnāvalī of Jāyasenāpati, 2.336(b).

28 N.S., 9.91, 9th chapter deals with gestures of hands.

29 N.S., 9.61.

30 N.S., 4.93, one hand stretched across the body, one foot kept on toes and the other hand held near the ear in allapallava-hasta is lalita karaṇa.

31 N.S., 4.133 (73rd karaṇa).

32 N.S., 4.85 (25th karaṇa).

33 N.S., 4.94 (34th karaṇa).

34 N.S., 9, 203.

35 Now preserved at Allahabad Museum, this is one of the most beautiful examples.

36 Epigraphica Indica, 5, p. 144.

37 One leg raised backward like a scorpion's tail, is vṛshchika pāda.

38 Where the vṛshcikapāda touches the forehead it is lalāta-tilaka. But in the sculpture it is represented most of the time, erect without any bend in which position it is identified by scholars as ūrdhvatāṇṇdava. Technically, however, this pose is close to vidutbhrānta karaṇa (64), N.S., 4.125.

39 The Sanskrit Buddhist Literature of Nepal, R. Mitra, Calcutta 1882, quoted by Getty, op. cit., p.37.

40 Iconography of Buddhist and Brahmanical Sculptures in the Dacca Museum, N.K.Bhattasali, Dacca, 1929, pl. xix.

41 Getty, Gaṇesha, p. 38.

42 Getty, Gaṇesha, p. 38, pl. 20(a).

43 Sylvain Levi, Le Nepal, Vol.II, p. 345 near Zimpi-Tandu an ancient temple is dedicated to Gaṇesha, dating roughly from 8th to 10th centuries.

44 See, Dhaki, "Shaiva images from Nepal", Discourses on Shiva, p. 32 to 37, pl. 47.

45 Ibid. Pl. 48.

46 K. Deva, “Images of Nepal”, Discourses on Shiva, Pl. 49.

47 Getty, Gaṇesha, p. 38.

48 Shivaramamurti, op. cit., p. 357, fig. 14.

49 Ibid, p. 357, fig. 15.

The Jātaka and Self-sacrifice

Musashi Tachikawa

I

The idea of transmigration had already been established by the seventh or sixth century B.C. when the early Upanishads were compiled, before the birth of Śākyamuni. This means that this idea was current among the common people while Śākyamuni was alive in the fifth or fourth century B.C.. However, Śākyamuni did not pay attention to the idea of transmigration, refusing to accept the belief that a person's soul passes into another body at death and thus exists forever. Contrary to the stance of the founder, however, the idea of transmigration came to form the basis of Buddhist thought. Generally speaking, this idea also came to be accepted in Hinduism.

Believers in transmigration hold that all living things will be reborn after death, or rather, after the expiration of their body. If rebirth is to take place, there must be a certain permanent something that passes from the dead body to the new body. Most of

Buddhists believe that rebirth is driven by the power of karma which results from the deeds one has done in this life. Karma refers to all the potential power stemming from one's actions and consequences of those actions. It is believed that the power of the actions one has done in this life will remain even after the expiration of the body, and result in rebirth in a new body.

Hindus, especially Brahmins, in general, believe in the existence of a soul while Buddhists tend to attribute the cause of rebirth to the power of karma. In both cases, the idea of transmigration is underlain by the belief that a certain permanent something continues to exist even after the death of the body, and that it takes possession of a succession of new bodies with the death of the old one.

The idea of transmigration underwent gradual transformation as it was introduced to Tibet and China with the spread of Buddhism. While the conventional belief held that the soul would acquire a new body just as we would take off old clothes and put on new ones,. people came to place greater importance on the relation between the old body and the new body. Buddhists, from the beginning, have not believed in a soul, and thought transmigration was driven by karma, i.e., actions and their consequences. Therefore, they felt that the body was more closely related to karma than it was to a soul. According to their reasoning, it is karma in the present life that determines the body in which a person will be reborn in the next life. If one does good things, he/she will be reborn at a higher level or into a higher status in the next life. Bad conduct though will result in retribution in the next life. Over time, this belief has come to constitute the core of Buddhist ethics.

There is often doubt as to whether transmigration actually takes place or not. Whether it does or not will remain an eternal mystery. At least one can say with certainty that no one can answer this question in a manner that satisfies everyone. In spite of this uncertainty, the idea of transmigration has continued to captivate people almost for 3,000 years. This is because everyone knows that human beings are doomed to death, or, at least, to the expiration of their current bodies.

Once born, all living things grow and eventually die. There are no exceptions. Following the pattern incorporated in cells of living organic bodies, they are destined to undergo the process of birth, growth and death as they continue to take nourishment. According to the *Taittirīya Upaniṣad* (3.1.1), one of the early Upanishads, it is *brahman* (the basic principle of the universe) "from which these living things are born, by which, when born they live, into which when dying, they enter ."[1] In a later age, Hindu gods such as Viṣṇu are believed to share the functions of that fundamental principle called "*brahman* ."[2]

From a seed, shoots emerge and young leaves sprout. Then the leaves become proliferate, fruits are produced, and, eventually, the plant withers. Dogs, cats, and all people start life as cute babies but are destined to reach an old age. While plants, animals, and people alike repeat the same cycle of birth, growth, and death, there may be something—a source of life—that remains in existence unaffected by these changes, and that constitutes the principle of the universe. Most Hindus think. in this manner.

This thought is underlain by the hope that the expiration of present bodies of people will not mean the end of their selves or lives. One can attain immortality simply through the belief that even after the death of our body, something—whether or not it be a soul—continues to exist forever, or, as long as this world lasts. In this sense, the idea of transmigration can be seen as a means of teaching us that the soul that dwells in (or possesses) a short-lived body has eternal life. The death of the body is a necessary step in order for the soul to pass into a new body. If one can acquire new bodies one after another, he/she will never meet death.

Hindus usually cremate the corpse. For them, one may be allowed to say that the body to be cremated is no more important than old, worn-out clothes. Hindus usually do not display a strong attachment to their existing body in the stage of transmigration, but they hope to acquire a new body, no matter what shape it may have, and the final liberation from transmigration. Many Hindus believe that they will be immortal as long as they remain in the cycle of transmigration in this world. Buddhists as well hope to pass into a new body after death. Mahayana Buddhists in Katmandu and Tibetan Buddhists generally hope to be reborn in their next life into a body at a higher level or with a higher status.

II

Nevertheless, the ultimate goal of Buddhism is to attain final liberation (*mokṣa*). This means that the freeing of oneself from transmigration which is full of pain. In ancient India, Buddhism was basically a religion for groups of monks who gave up their worldly lives. By withdrawing from the world, these monks tried to free themselves from most of the bonds of clan and family, which constituted an important part of their transmigrating lives.

The final liberation means deliverance from transmigration which is the process of the power of karma (or a soul) to acquire a new bodies one after another. For Buddhists, however, Nirvana is the highest bliss, "It is not a negative state of annihilation but a positive state of joy, consciousness grown from an unhappy to a beatific one,"[3] On the other hand, "the Hindu affirms that man can realize his identity with Brahman, the ground of all beings."[4] In Sanskrit, the body is *deha* and the soul that passes from one body to another is *dehin*, meaning something that possesses a body. This shows that the soul is believed to be the owner of a body. The *Bhagavadgītā* (2.22), one of the most important Hindu scriptures, tells us, "As a man throws away worn-out garments and wears other new ones, the soul (*dehin*) casts off its worn-out bodies and attains other new ones."[5] If we use this metaphor, final liberation can be compared to a body that no longer needs clothes.

Śākyamuni is considered to be the one whose life is the last. Buddha appearing in Aśvaghoṣa in the *Buddhacarita* (1,15) says, "This is my last birth in this world."[6] Born as a prince of the Śākyas, he attained Enlightenment at the age of thirty-six, and entered Parinirvāṇa at the age of eighty. The life of Śākyamuni as such was the final time for him to be born with a body in the cycle of transmigration. It is believed that the power of his karma left his body permanently—or he attained final liberation—when he entered Nirvana.

While Śākyamuni taught his disciples to perform practices to achieve final liberation, it is doubtful whether the direct disciples of

Śākyamuni, as well as Buddhist priests of later ages, really pursued final liberation that entailed the complete separation from their bodies. Of course, some ascetics actually destroyed their own bodies in pursuit of this goal. Apart from these few cases, however, common people generally do not wish to abandon their body even though this world is full of pain. In fact, almost all of the Nepali and Tibetan Buddhists whom I had the chance to interview replied that they would like to remain in the cycle of transmigration rather than being freed from it.

Śākyamuni, however, abandoned his kingdom and family to follow the path to final liberation. Tibetan and Nepali Buddhist yogis also cast off all their worldly ties to devote themselves to practices such as meditation. By so doing, they hope to free themselves from transmigration. However, only the founder of Buddhism and saints could follow such a difficult path, and one may say with near certainty that general believers are moving towards the opposite direction. While they are aware that Śākyamuni taught the importance of final liberation, they elect to remain in the cycle of transmigration to enjoy the worldly pleasures. The difference between the attitude of the founder and a few elite and that of general believers represents an inconsistency between the ideal and reality common in almost all religions. This inconsistency is mothered by the *jātaka*, the accounts of the previous lives of Śākyamuni, which are the main motif of the wall paintings in the Ajanta Caves.

The term "*jātaka*" literally means that which has been born. The word "*jāta*" is the past participle of the verb *jan,* and means that which has been born. The meaning of the suffix "*-ka*" is unclear. In the course of time, the word "*jātaka*" came to mean accounts of the previous lives of Śākyamuni.

After the death of Śākyamuni, his teachings were recorded in scriptures written in a Prakrit language called Pāli. The term *jātaka* was not used in the earlier version of these scriptures, which were written no later than about one-hundred and fifty years after the death of Śākyamuni, and few stories of the previous lives of Śākyamuni are contained in those scriptures. Of course, Śākyamuni could not have related the stories of his previous lives himself, because he denied the existence of former lives, not to mention the memories of them. After the passing of Śākyamuni, however, Buddhists produced many stories of his previous lives which generally began with the sentence, "the Master (Śākyamuni) told the story of his previous life as a bodhisattva as follows."

A Buddhist artifact in central India, the *stūpa* of Bharhut, dating from around the first century B.C., features more than twenty relief sculptures on its railing. These sculptures depict scenes from the stories of the previous lives of Śākyamuni, and the word "*jātaka* "is inscribed on some relief sculptures.[7] The scenes from the *jātaka* are also used as a motif of the relief sculptures of the great *stūpa* of Sanchi in central India and the *stūpa* of Amaravati in south India,[8] both constructed before the birth of Christ. These facts suggest that the *jātaka* were already so widely known as stories of the previous lives of Śākyamuni by around the first century B.C..

In general, *jātaka* today means a collection of 547 tales written in Pāli. The compilation of the tales is believed to have been completed around 500 A.D.. This collection of tales cannot be considered as Buddhist scriptures in the strict sense, and has been treated as a supplement to the scriptures. It should be noted, however, that most of these tales were developed from ancient *jātaka* found scattered throughout various canons of early Buddhism.

Buddhism has only a very limited number of myths, and the *jātaka* are representative of these Buddhist myths. Hinduism, to the contrary, is known for its abundance of myths. Myths about Hindu deities are reflected everywhere—in trees and flowers along the street, as well as in mountains and rivers. Or rather, one could say that Hindus believe that mountains, rivers, and trees themselves are sacred deities. Myths called Buddhist myths actually should not exist, in light of the fact that Śākyamuni, the founder, is a historical figure, and that he did not believe in the existence of God or the creator of the universe. In later ages, however, Buddhists grew increasingly interested in developing myths. Then, Śākyamuni, although a historical figure, came to be depicted as a superhuman being that accumulated merits in his past lives and attained Enlightenment in his final life. By the same process, he was also believed to have had memories of his past lives.

The *jātaka* do not relate complex philosophical ideas. Instead, they incorporate easy-to-understand fables that were widely known at the time of their compilation. Mahayana Buddhism which began to prevail around the first century A.D. formulated an elaborate philosophical system by the seventh century A.D.. In its scriptures, Śākyamuni, given the status of a superhuman being or a deity, discusses complex philosophical doctrines to guide disciples. Even priests with academic backgrounds have difficulty understanding these doctrines. But, in the *jātaka*, Śākyamuni speaks to people in a much easier manner using simple fables, though he is still depicted as a superhuman being.

III

The *jātaka* are based on the principle that good conduct brings positive results, while bad conduct results in retribution. The merit accumulated in his past lives brought Śākyamuni a substantial reward in the same life. Moreover, his good deeds ultimately produced the greatest result—Enlightenment and Nirvana, which Śākyamuni attained in the life he began as a Śākya prince. His most highly rewarded deed was renunciation—giving up the princely life to become a wandering yogi. By discarding his noble status, family, and by even abandoning his duty to protect his kingdom, Śākyamuni could attain Enlightenment and Nirvana.

The word Nirvana (*nirvāṇa*) literally means extinction. According to this meaning, Nirvana refers to the extinction of impure thoughts and actions that we cannot prevent as long as one's life lasts. Śākyamuni, who achieved Enlightenment, discarded his body to enter Parinirvāṇa at the age of eighty. The Nirvana that

Śākyamuni attained at the end of his life provides the starting point of every *jātaka,* because the merits recounted in the tales which Śākyamuni accumulated in his past lives as a bodhisattva were all directed toward Nirvana. The compilers of the tales arranged the stories backwards, starting from the time of Śākyamuni's entrance in to Nirvana.

In arranging these stories, the compilers dramatically emphasized Śākyamuni's renunciation. Something must be sacrificed if something new is to be born. In this sense, renunciation is a kind of sacrifice made to produce something else. The compilers of the *jātaka* regarded renunciation as self-sacrifice on the part of Śākyamuni. The tales show various forms of self-sacrifice, such as the sacrifice of both his eyes,[9] in addition to renunciation.

The Ajanta Caves have many wall paintings that depict scenes from the *jātaka*. The main theme of these paintings is self-sacrifice, as demonstrated by the paintings of the renunciation of the Prince in Cave 1 (a scene from "The Birth of Mahājanaka")[10] and of the sacrifice of his own body in Cave 17 (a scene from "The Tale of an Elephant").[11] Not a few *jātaka* feature characters who were not only of a generous nature, but who also sacrificed excessively and even masochistically. While there are fables that teach us not to trust others, many of the tales emphasize the importance of self-sacrifice for saving others.

IV

Some of the *jātaka* are about betrayers who meet with misfortune, such as "The Tale of an Ape" depicted in Cave 17.[12] In this tale, Śākyamuni lives the life of an ape. One day, the ape found a farmer who had fallen from a cliff and helped him. While the exhausted ape was sleeping, the farmer threw a stone at the ape in an attempt to kill it because he wanted to eat the ape. The ape narrowly escaped and ran into a forest. Later, the farmer contracted a fever and pus came out of every part of his body. He then became aware that he had committed the sin of betrayal. At that moment, he descended into hell. This story tells us that the vicious deed of betrayal deserves the tortures of hell.

Why did the farmer go to hell? Who punished him? Buddhism has no deities to punish or curse people. Hence, the farmer himself invited retribution upon himself through his vicious deed. The deeds (karma) one does drive transmigration from one life to another. All existing things are the result of accumulated past deeds: good deeds result in reward, and bad deeds in retribution.

Then, if one kills a living thing, must he be reborn in hell? How about warriors whose duty is to kill their enemies in battlefields, and farmers who have to kill insects in their fields? Are they all bound for hell? In case of the *jātaka* above, the farmer was sent to hell because he betrayed the ape that saved his life. Why does betrayal deserve punishment in hell?

One may say that nowadays every human being is walking on ice covering chaos where ethics, morals, and religions are rendered powerless. Everyone is actually treading on thin ice. Through the ice, we can see the rapid current below. As long as people are aware that killing is a bad deed, there can be some hope. However, there are some people who enjoy the act of killing with little or no remorse. It seems that our modern society is producing an increasing number of these people.

Buddhism teaches us that existence is suffering. Suffering (Pali: *dukkha*) does not mean mere mental or physical suffering, but refers to a bad or unavoidable *(dukh)* fate *(kha)*. This teaching puts a stress on the fact that our society is based on something horrible, which is how Śākyamuni and those who pursued Buddhism in later ages viewed the depths of human beings.

V

What can we do to prevent people from breaking through the thin ice in their desperate pursuit of self-interest? The answer to this question in the *jātaka* was self-sacrifice. First, the renunciation by the prince of the Śākyas is regarded as self-sacrifice offered for the good of other people, even though it bewildered Śākyamuni's wife and others related to him. The painting in Cave 1 in Ajanta depicts the story of King Mahājanaka who withdrew from the world. This story was modeled on the renunciation by the prince of the Śākyas whose path to Enlightenment started at the moment of his renunciation.

Not all *jātaka* are about sacrificing one's self for the sake of others, many of them have a motif of self-sacrifice such as the story of the white elephant with six tusks depicted in Cave 17 in Ajanta . This elephant offered its six tusks to a hunter, resigning itself to death.

Offering one's life to save others constitutes the climax of the *jātaka*, which also parallels the climax of the life of the Śākya prince who later attained Enlightenment and became the Buddha, the Enlightened One. All the past lives of Śākyamuni converge in Nirvana, the end of the last life. Cave 26 of Ajanta features a statue seven meters long of the reclining Buddha as he prepares to enter Nirvana.[13] This cave has no wall paintings depicting the worldly lives of the common people and only silence surrounds the *stūpa* and the statue of the Buddha.

Śākyamuni searched for deliverance from transmigration. It has been people's belief that Śākyamuni achieved the final liberation when he attained the state of Nirvana. However, it seems that most common people have not been serious about attaining the final liberation themselves. Perhaps, most of them would opt to remain in the cycle of transmigration even if they have to live as an animal or a bird in their next life.

Then, why is Śākyamuni believed to have attained the final liberation when he entered Nirvana? Why did he free himself from transmigration in spite of the fact common people do not wish to do so? Here, we can see an inconsistency common to almost all religions. Saints are expected to achieve even greater results because common people do not wish to do so themselves. By so doing, these saints can contribute to the happiness of the common people. The prince of the Śākyas staged the ultimate story in his last life. It is the Buddhist belief the Śākyamuni offered his death for their good.

Śākyamuni, Gautama Buddha, dedicated his body and heart which had lived for eighty years as sacrifice to time, the monster that controls transmigration, just as the rabbit jumped into the fire to offer its meat.[14] With his renunciation, Śākyamuni attempted a great feat which the common people did not wish to do, and even if they wished to, could not achieve. People worship the life of Buddha, developed myths called *jātaka*, and worship the Buddha as a saint who embodied their ideal and as one who attained a state which they themselves can never attain. One may say that the life of Buddha was offered on a sacrificial altar.

Bibliography

Behl, Benoy K., *The Ajanta Caves, Ancient Paintings of Buddhist India,* Thames and Hudson, 1998.

Belvalkar, Shripad Krishna, *The Bhagavadgītā,* Bhandarkar Oriental Research Institute, Poona, 1968.

Cowell, E.B.(ed.), *The Jataka or Stories of the Buddha's Former Births,* Vol.I (tr. by Robert Charles); Vol.II (tr. by W.H.D. Rouse); Vol.III (tr. by H.T.Francis and R.A. Neil); Vol.IV (tr. by W.H.D. Rouse); Vol.V (tr. by H.T.Francis); Vol.VI (tr. by E.B. Cowell and W.H.D. Rouse), The Pali Text Society, London, Boston and Henley, 1891 (rept. of 1895).

Cunningham, A., *The Stupa of Bharhut, A Buddhist Monument, Ornamented with Numerous Sculptures,* London, 1879.

Higata, Ryuushou, *Jātaka Gaisetsu (General View of Jātaka),* Suzuki Foundation, Tokyo, 1961.

Johnston, E.H., *The Buddhacarita or Acts of the Buddha,* Motilal Banarsidass, Delhil, Patna, Varanasi, 2 parts, 1972 (rept.1936).

Kashyap, J. Bhikku, *The Paṇṇhāna* (ParteVI) *Nalandā-Devanāgari- Pāli Series,* Pali Publication Board, 1961.

Kern, H.(ed.) *Jātakamālā, (Harvard Oriental Series 1),* Boston, 1891.

Radhakrishnan, S., *The Principal Upaniṣads*, Humanities Paperback Library, Atloantic Highlands, NJ, 1978 (rept.1953)

Schlingloff, Dieter, *Erzählende Wandmalereien, Narrative Wall-paintings*, 1,Vol.I,Interpretation, 1,Vol.II Supplement, Arrassowitz Verlag, Wiesbaden, 2000.

Speyer, J.S.(tr.), *Jātakamālā, Sared Books of East*, Vol.1, London, 1895.

Tachikawa, Musashi, *Ajanta to Erora (Ajanta and Ellora)*, (photographed by Tsugusato Omura), Shieisha, Tokyo, 2000.

Takata, Osamu, *Ajanta, Cave-temples and Murals*, (photographed by Mikihiro Taeda) Heibonsha, Tokyo, 1971.

Yazdani, G., *Ajanta, The Colour and Monochrome Reproductions of the Ajanta Frescoes Based on Photography*, Oxford University Press, London, Part I, 1930; Part II, 1933; Part III, 1946; Part IV, 1955.

Notes

1 Radhakrishnan 1978: 553.

2 Belvarkar 1968: 19, 31.

3 Kashyap 1961:iii.

4 Ibid:iii.

5 Belvarkar 1968: 9.

6 Johnston 1972: Part I, 2.

7 Cf. Cunningham 1879: Pl.3, Fig.4 Higata 1961: 53.

8 Cf. Schlingloff 2000: Vol. II, 24.

9 Cf. Sivi-Jātaka, No.499 Cowell 1891: IV, 250-256. For mural paintings of this story, see Yazdani 1955: Part IV, Pls.LXVc, LXV,a-c, Behl 1998: 227, Tachikwa 2000: 40.

10 Cf.Mahājanaka-Jātaka, No.539 Cowell 1891: VI,19-37. For mural paintings of this story, see Takata 11971: Pls.80-89, Schlingloff 2000: Vol. I, 217-221.

11 Hasti-Jātaka,*Jātakamālā*,No.30 Kern1891:No.30, For mural paintings of this story, see Yazdani1942: Part III,Pl.48b,49, Schlingloff 2000: Vol.I,120-123. Tachikwa 2000: 41.

12 Vanara-Jātaka, No.516 Cowell 1891: V,37-41. For mural paintings of this story, see Yazdani 1955: Part IV,Pl.29, Behl 1998: 192-193, Tachikwa 2000: 35.

13 Cf. Tachikwa 2000: 48-49.

14 Sasa-Jātaka,No.316 Cowell 1891: III, 34-37.

Environment Perspective of Hindu Festivals

N. Vijaya

Nature being the source of sustenance and survival, men first worshipped Nature as Goddess. This fact is true to almost all ancient civilizations of the world.

In his work "Man's Responsibility for Nature", Pass More discussed in detail the element of Nature worship and the methods adopted for the protection of Nature embodied in the ancient European culture. Even in the modern times, according to Pass More, the European intellectuals and thinkers displayed their love for Nature through the Romantic arts and Romantic poetry.[1]

In India, the ancient Indian Culture is reflected in the four Vedas, which are the sacred scriptures for the Hindus. The prayers and hymns invoking for the mercy of such elemental forces of Nature *Prithivi* (The Earth Goddess), *Agni* (Fire God), *Varuṇa* (The God of Rain and Water) amply illustrate the practice of Nature worship prevalent among Hindus. For instance, Ṛgveda, the oldest among the Vedas, begins with an invocation of seasons caused by the passage of time and the distinction of each season, especially that of the spring season.[2] Further, the following invocations are found in the Yajurveda:

> O! Waters! You are the source of happiness and comfort. For our sake you bear food. Bless us with a sublime and splendid vision.

> O earth: you bring us joy and comfort. You favor us by providing with a dwelling place. You are universally acclaimed. Bless us with happiness and comfort.

Thus it is clear that these invocational prayers in the Vedas bear a testimony to the Nature worship that was in vogue among the ancient Hindus and to the fact that recognition of the elements of Nature as the sustaining source for the survival of the living organism. Worshipping them as Gods and Goddesses was a very ancient tradition among the Hindus.

However, after the entry of the concept of religion into men's minds, there appeared to have been changes in the phenomenon of Nature worship in different civilizations. As pointed out by Lymn White Jr., an American historian in his book "Roots of the Ecological Crisis"[5] during the Pre-Christian era in the European Culture (i.e. before the propagation of Christianity) there was a widespread practice of worshipping trees and other objects of nature as presiding deities, and therefore Nature was not attacked and destroyed. But in the later period, this Pre-Christian Culture was labeled as paganism resulting in a loss of faith in the Pagan Gods and Goddesses and this change led to an indiscriminate invasion and plundering of Nature.[6] Therefore, it can be stated that the cultures of all human communities in the world began with Nature worship.

In contrast, in the Modern period the influence of religion became dominant and consequently the worship of religious prophets gained priority leading to an unfortunate disregard for the worship of Nature.[7] But fortunately Hindus have still continued their devotion to Nature and have preserved their practices of Nature worship. Worshipping the different forms and objects of Nature as Gods and Goddesses is found among the Hindus, even today.

In the Hindu way of life, religion, custom, tradition, culture, holidays, festivals and celebrations all are synthesized into the worship of Nature. All these festivals and celebrations are incorporated into the factors of human health, environmental protection, hygiene of living places, and these factors are coordinated into memorable events i.e. festivals.

The Hindu tradition has recognized the periodical changes in Nature, which are manifested in the form of different seasons and the accompanying changes in the environment; and therefore the Hindus welcome the advent of each season with joy. A number of festivals are conducted in the Hindu community to mark the change of seasons and the changes in the environment. For instance, *Ugadi* (New Year's day), *Saṅkarānthi* (Harvest Festival), *Holi* (which marks the beginning of spring) etc. are seasonal in orientation. These festive occasions illustrate the environmental awareness of the Hindus.

The Ṛgveda describes the spring season as the king of seasons among the six seasons viz. *Vasanta* (Spring), *Grișma* (Summer), *Varșa* (The rainy season), *Śarat* (Autumn), *Hemanta* (The season of mist) and *Sisira* (Winter).

Vasantotsava (the festival of Spring) is celebrated by Hindus with great mirth and merriment. As it occurs in the month of *Chaitra* this spring festival is also known as *Chaitrotsava* (The festival of *Chaitra*). In North India, this festival is popularly known as "*Holi*". In the spring season, the entire Nature turns colourful and sonorous with beautiful sights and sounds, together with fully blossomed flowers and melodious songs of birds like Parrots, Cuckoos and Larks. Holi is celebrated to mark this blowing beauty of Nature as a part of the Hindu Nature worship. In addition, seasons have an impact on the human mind. It is believed that especially the spring season generates the emotions of love and amours feelings in people. Hence, *Holi* is also called *Madanamahotsava* (Festival of the God of love). On this festive occasion of *Holi*, men and women dance and sing merrily, sprinkle on each other with coloured water mixed with turmeric and lime powder called *Vasantham* and freely express their feelings of love and lust.[8] Turmeric powder and lime powder act like powerful pesticides and by sprinkling water mixed with these powders prevents a variety of skin diseases. Thus, this festive act helps people to keep good health. Ironically, the modern people today are causing skin diseases to themselves by unwisely using chemically produced cosmetics and coloured pastes and powders.

Another important festival for Hindus is *Ugādi* i.e. the New Year day. It is reported that the Pharsees also celebrate this festival like the Hindus.[9] They call this festival *Narvoz* (the New day). On the Ugādi day Hindus eat a kind of "*Chetny*" called *Ugādi pachadi* (in Tegulu). This *Chetny* or Paste is prepared with fresh tamarind, pieces of fresh green mango, *neem* flowers, new *jiggery*, Salt and fresh chilly (*mirchi*) powder which provide the six basic taste (*Shadruchulu*). That is, it made up of all the floral and vegetable ingredients, which are abundantly available in Nature on the advent of New Year. During this time, the entire nature sheds her garb of old leaves and wears colourful robes of new leaves, flowers, twigs and green fruits. It may be mentioned here that the consumption of *neem* flowers destroys worms in the stomach; thus, the *Ugādi Pachaḍi* is like a seasonal medicine and contributes to the general health of people.

Another important Hindu festival is *Saṅkrānthi*. This festival is based on the movement of the Sun in the firmament. The sun travels southwards for six months, and then it travels to the north. The northward journey of the sun is known as *Makara Saṇkramaṇa* (entry into the house of Capricorn). This day of *Saṅkramaṇa* is celebrated as *Saṇkrānthi* festival. During the season when *Saṅrānthi* is celebrated, the nights are longer and it is cold. Hence giving gifts like sesame, ghee and woolen rugs to the poor people is as widely followed custom on this festive occasion. It is worthy to note that the three items mentioned here are heat generating and useful to protect people from the winter bite. Further, during the season of *Saṅkrānthi* festival, people whitewash their houses and decorate their front yards with splendid colourful patterns using flour and lime powder. These festive activities reflect the spirit of Nature worship and environmental hygiene.

A major festival of the Hindus is *Daśara*. It is celebrated for nine days during the season of *Śarath*. *Dassara* celebrations reflect the age-old culture and tradition of the Hindus. In the pre-historic times, when Hindus were primarily an agrarian community they worshipped the trees as a symbol of the fertility of earth.[10] The seed lying dormant in the layers of the soil, sprouts into a sapling and grows gradually into a great tree. The pre-historic Hindus realized that this phenomenon was made possible by the fertility of the earth and considered the tree as a symbolic representation of the Goddess. This tree is useful to man from the medical point of view.[11]

On the *Vijayadaśami* day (i.e. the tenth day of *Daśara* festival) Hindus not only worship the '*Sami* Tree but also look at a bird called *Palapitta* because they consider that doing these two things brings them happiness and prosperity. These two facts can be considered to reflect the Hindu concern for environmental protection, i.e. the protection of the flora and fauna in the Nature.

Besides worshipping Nature according to the cycle of seasons, Hindus also consider everything in this created world as divine manifestations and worship it. Hindu festivals like *Śītalasaptami*, *Tulasi Vratam*, *Nagula Chavithi*, *Vinayaka Chavithi*, *Garuda Panchami* and *Hanumanjayanthi* illustrate this tradition.

Another prominent feature of the India folk culture is to consider an entire village as an environmental unit and to assign a village deity to the protection of that unit from environmental, natural and health hazards. The *neem* tree in the village taken as the symbolic representative of that particular tradition is the rural life of India.[12] The symbolic significance of the worship of different forms of Nature in the forms of a variety of village deities has assumed different manifestation.

Many village deities and Goddesses like *Talamma* are worshipped even today as the presiding deities of fertility and crops. Deities like *Gangamma* and *Maisamma* are worshipped as presiding deities of tanks and other sources of water and irrigation. Those like *maremma* and *polemma* are worshipped as deities presiding over such epidemic and endemic diseases like measles and cholera.

Further village Goddesses like *Ankalmma, Mahankali, Laxmamma* and *Sitalamma* are worshipped as protectors of the entire village from all natural calamities. All these Goddesses are worshipped by Hindus collectively. They look upon the *neem* tree as the symbol for all these Goddesses and worship the *neem* with devotion.[13]

It is proverbially said the benefits from the *neem* tree are thousand-fold. This tree has the highest medical quality because all of its parts have some curative value. For instance, the oil drawn from the *neem* seed cures skin diseases, while its bark is used to reduce bodily heat and temperature, and the *neem* flowers can kill the worms in the stomach, whereas the *neem* leaves are used in the treatment of small-pox and also to drive away mosquitoes and other such insects. The *neem* shade provides a cool shelter while the breeze from the *neem* branches is an antidote for environmental pollution.[14] In this way the *neem* tree protects man like a mother. Hence this tree is respected and loved as a mother and worshipped as a Goddess. The *neem* worship is performed by the Hindus in the month of April when the summer starts to cool the atmosphere. This festival of *neem* worship is known by different names in different regions of India.[15] In Bengal it is known as "*Śītala Saptami*", in Rajasthan as the festival of "*Yella*" and in the *Telangana* region "*Batukamma*" festival. This festival is intended to propagate the importance of the *neem* tree as an environmental balancer in the summer and a controller of pollution apart from its medicinal value.

The Hindus also consider the *neem* tree as a symbol for *Śakti* (Goddess of Energy), and the *Tulasi* for *Lazmi* (Goddess of Wealth) and grow these trees in their courtyards and backyards respectively. Hindus women worship the *Tulsi* every day in the morning. On a special festival day of *Karthika Suddha Dwadasi* (December) they worship *Tulsi* plant and this holy day is known as *Tulsivratham* or *Ksheerabdhi Vratam*.

There is a popular mythological episode called "*Krishnatulābaram,*" which highlights the importance of *Tulsi*, as summarized below.

Once, Sage Narada requested Satyabhama for Srikrishna to have gifted to Narada himself. Then later in an effort to get back *Srikrishna* she offered valuable things equal to his weight and started weighing him in a large balance. *Srikrishna* was sitting on one pan and she started filling the other with gold. Even after putting as much gold as she could the pan with gold weighed lighter where Srikrishna weighed much heavier than the gold. Greatly frustrated she sought the intervention of *Rukmini* (the first wife of Srikrishna). Then Rukmini cleared the pan of the balance with gold and placed on it with one *Tulsi dala* (a balance (bunch) of leaves). Then Srikrishna became as light as cotton and his pan went up immediately. This story reveals the fact that a few leaves of *Tulsi* are more powerful even than Srikrishna who is considered as an incarnation of God. This episode symbolically implies that health is more than wealth and hence a health-giver greater than gold equal to the weight of a person.

The *Tulsi* Plant has the greatest medicinal value. It purifies the air in the atmosphere and thereby prevents air pollution.[16] It is a very useful plant not only for the protection of environment but also for human health. In the Ayurveda (Indian Indigenous Medicine) and in several *Purāaṇas*, *Tulsi* is described as a distinguished plant and that it can be used as a medicine for a number of diseases. It also can be used as an appetizer, a remedy for skin diseases, a medicine for kidney problems, a traditional remedy to clear phlegm, and an antidote for snake bite.[17]

Another ancient feature of Hindus Culture is the worship of snakes. The practice of snake worship can be traced back to the Vedic times as attested by the prayers to snakes mentioned in the Vedas.[18] Snakes have their habitat on the corn fields, the villages, and even the dwelling places of human beings. There is a strong possibility that they bite people and cause death. Therefore, in the early stages of history, people started worshipping snakes out of the fear for life, but later they realized that snakes positively contribute to ecological balance and protect the crops. Frogs make holes in the corn fields and rats and mice burrow these holes further and live there. These rodents eat and destroy every corn seed right from plantation to harvest. Snakes eat frogs, rats and other rodents and thus indirectly help the farmers and save the crops. So Hindus worship the snakes not only with fear of them but also with a sense of devotion and affection. This festival of snake worship is known as *Nagula Chavithi*.(nāga cathurti) On this festive occasion Hindus go to the ant hills, habitats of snakes, worship them by offering milk and other eatables with great devotion.

Among Hindu festivals, which are intended for environmental protection and ecological balance, *Vinayaka Chavithi* (or *Ganesha Chathurthi*) is a very important one. For Hindus Vinayaka is the presiding God of paddy. He travels on the back of a rat, which is an enemy to the crops and paddy. Thus, Lord Vinayaka controls rats and protects the crops in the fields. He is worshipped with 21 varieties of plant's leaves and herbs like *Darbha*, *Garika*, *Bilva*, *Sami*, *Aswatha*, *Danimma*, *Jilledu*, *Ummetta*, and flowers like *Zazi*, *Kaluva*, *Dasani* and *Mogali*. All these Trees, plants and flowers are available in our neighborhood. All these are described in the Ayurveda (i.e. India Indigenous medicine) as having medical value.[19]

This tradition of worshipping Lord Vinayaka came into prominence to enable people to identify and protect the trees, plants and herbs, which contribute to the up-keep of their health and to preserve this knowledge for generations. Further, it may be stated that this tradition imbibes the spirit of environmental protection and ecological balance.

Hindus celebrate a number of festivals every year. On the full month of *Śrāvaṇ* the *Ganga* river is worshipped to atone the ten sins of men (*Dasahara*). This festival is known as *Gangotsava*. On the festival of *Aśokashaṣṭhi*, the Asoka tree is worshipped. Likewise the *Aśwattha* tree is worshipped on *Somavaravratha* festival, the bird eagle is worshipped on *Garudapanchami*, the great monkey Hanuman is worshipped on *Hanumanjayanthi*. The Sun God is worshipped on *Rathasapthami* festival and the domestic animals like crows, buffalos and bulls on the *Kanuma* day i.e. the day after *Saṅkrānthi*. Apart from this, each and every God and Goddess of Hindus culture has an animal as their vehicle, which are equally adored and worshipped. This shows that Hindus have a lot of respect and regard for all the creatures of the world. But in the west, man is considered to be the only one who can make use of each and every aspect of the nature for his own enjoyment.

All these festivals organized in the Hindu tradition are arranged in a systematic manner to show their respect, love and devotion to the Nature. These festivals are symbolic reflections of the interest evinced and the care taken by Hindus to protect the environment and to maintain the ecological balance in Nature.

A Glossary of Botanical Names

Sami: (Jammi)	–	Orosopis specigera
Nimba (Vepa)	–	Azadirachta Indica
Tulasi	–	Ocimum Sanctum
Darbha	–	Eragrostis Cynasuroives
Asoka	–	Sarca Indica
Bila	–	Aegle marmelos
Aswattha	–	Ficus religiosa
Dadima (Danimma)		
Arkapatra (Jilledu)		
Dhattura (Ummatta)	–	Datura metal
Devadara	–	Cedrus deodara
Vishunu Kranta	–	Convolvulus Pluricaulis
Apamarga (Uttareni)	–	Achyranathes Aspera
Kutaja (Thummi)	–	Holarrhena
Durrva	–	Cynodon dactylon

Marruvam	–	Orgamum Majorana
Karavera (Ganneru)	–	Nelium Odorum
Kovidara (De Vekanchana)	–	Bauhinia Purpurea
Aranvadha (Regu)	–	Cassia Fistula
Kapittha (Velaga)	–	Wood apple

Reference Books

A reference guide to Ayurvedic Practice (English) Dr. Ch. Murali Manohar – Publication Division, Raksha Aryuvedics, Hyderabad (1996).

Dhannvanthari Nighantu (Sanskrit) – Vavilla Rama Swami Sastrulu & Sons, Madras (1954).

Dravyaguna Vijnana (Vol II) (Hindi) Prof. P.V. Sharma – Choukamba Bharati Academy, Varanasi (1994).

Enadu – Adivaram (Telugu daily journal) 20-10-96.

Hinduvala Pandugalu (Telugu) - Suvararam Pratapa Reddy – Andhra Saraswatha Parishat, Hyderabad (1987).

Paryavarana Bharati – (Telugu Quarterly Journal) 605, Maheswari Complex, Masab Tank, Hyderabad (1994).

Sri Krishna Yajurveda – (Telugu) Translated by Ch. L. Narasimha Sastri, Laxmi Narasimha Press, Machilipatnam, (1988).

Telugu Lo Rutha Kavyalu (Telugu) C.V. Jaya Veera Raju Chenna Madhava Publishers, Peddapalli, Karimnagar Dist. 1989.

Notes

1 Paryavarana Bharathi (Telugu) March-June 1994 page 50.

2 Telugulo Ritukavyalu (Telugu) page 9.

3 Sri. Yajurveda (Sanskrit) page 135.

4 Ibid. page 188.

5 Paryavarana Bharathi (Telugu) March-June 1995 page 50.

6 Ibid.

7 Ibid.

8 Hinduvula Pandugalu (Telugu) pages 143,43.

9 Ibid.

10 Enadu (Sunday –Telugu Daily) 20-10-1996 page 24.

11 Hinduvula panduigula (Telugu) page 38.

12 Paryavarana Bharathi (Telugu) March-June 1994 page 51.

13 Ibid.

14 Ibid.

15 Ibid. – June-August 1994 page 46.

16 Hinduvula pandugalu – page 175.

17 Hinduvula Pandugalu (Telugu) page 82.

18 Ibid. pages 78-82.

19 Sri Yajurveda – pages 205, 209, 215.

20 Dhanvanthari Nighantuvu (Sanskrit) pages 52, 54, 80, 72, 96, 7.

Relevance of Mahatma Gandhi and His Thought in Modern Times

J. K. Bajaj

I. Gandhi – The Sanatani Hindu

Mahatma Gandhi was a seeker of truth. He pursued his seeking within the all-encompassing fold of Sanatana dharma, the timeless discipline, which the Indians believe is inherent in creation. His seeking and the discipline of his pursuit thus place him amongst the great divine personages of Indian tradition, whose life and teachings transcend the constraints of time and space, and remain perpetually relevant to mankind, especially for the Indians.

Ordinary Indians began to look upon Mahatma Gandhi as a divine personage as soon as he arrived in India on January 9, 1915, at the age of 46, after having spent many long years in South Africa struggling for the preservation of the basic human dignity of the Indians there. After arriving, he spent almost the whole of 1915 visiting different parts of the country and trying to comprehend the condition of India. During these visits he was everywhere given a reverential welcome. On June 17, within a week of his arrival, he visited Rajkot, in his native Saurashtra, and the people there insisted on pulling his carriage, as they would do for a divine personage. During the next few months, there were reports from places as far as Ahmedabad, Calcutta, Rangoon and Madras of people unharnessing horses from his carriage and drawing it .[1]

At all these places he was often addressed as the Mahatma, the great soul, the realised one. It seems the epithet was first used by the people in his native Saurashtra; soon he was being addressed thus almost everywhere, even in Gurukul Kangari, near Hardwar, in the north of India.[2] While in Hardwar, Mahatma Gandhi, greatly concerned with the condition of India and like a true follower of Sanatana dharma, imposed upon himself a high penance. On April 10, he took a vow that while in India, he would not eat more than five things in 24 hours and he would take no meal after sunset. Only water was excluded from the five things, but spices like cardamom and the like were included, and nut and its oil were to be counted as one of the things of the five. .[3]

Ordinary people who saw Mahatma Gandhi in person were certainly struck by his transparent divinity. A temple in Sitamarhi, the birthplace of Sri Sita, where also it was found that the ordinary people of India had the same understanding of the Mahatma as a divine personality . In the temple hall, opposite the main deity, Sri Rama with Sita and Lakshmana, they had put a statue of Hanuman on one pillar and of Mahatma Gandhi on the other, both of them standing in the posture of a humble devotee and servant, so characteristic of Hanuman.

Recalling the name of Sri Hanuman in the context of Mahatma Gandhi seems particularly significant, because like Hanuman, Mahatma Gandhi sought truth as a humble and unquestioningly devoted servant of Sanatana dharma. He was not interested merely in the abstractions of Sanatana dharma, and was not just devoted to *jñāanā*, knowledge, alone; on the other hand, he was equally devoted to the preservation and glory of the institutional framework through which Sanâtana dharma manifests in the Indian society and civilisation. According to Jagadguru Sankaracharya Sri Chandrasekharendra Saraswati of Kanchi Kamakoti Peetham, who depicts Mahatma Gandhi to the entirety of Sanatana dharma. Reviewing the state of dharma and the efforts to reform it during the British period, the Paramacharya wrote:[5]

Raja Rammohun Roy, the first in the field [of reform], being the founder of the Brahmo Samaj, saw no virtue in Hinduism other than the monotheistic philosophy of Brahman inculcated in the Upanishads. He condemned as weeds all other aspects of traditional Hinduism including Vedic karmanushthanas, idol worship, varna by birth and avataratatva. His was a time when the Christian missionaries in Bengal, with the nucleus of their educational institutions, the Presidency College, Calcutta, were rapidly weaning away educated Hindus from the religion of their forefathers. At that critical juncture, the Brahmo Samaj did yeoman service to Hinduism by averting the calamity. Yet it had to disown almost all the features of Hinduism that formed the basis of attack by the missionaries of alien faith.

Then came the Arya Samaj founded by Dayananda Saraswati in a somewhat different context. Hindus in north-west India were scattered among the aggressive Moslem majority and any reform there had to proceed on the lines of augmenting their numbers. The Muhammadans too had their ceremonials. But the principal target of their attack on Hinduism was idolatory. So the Arya Samaj was an unconscious improvement upon the previous Brahmo Samaj in as much as it did not disown Vedic rituals or Karma Kanda but laid much stress upon it. They condemned varna by birth, as it stood in the way of augmentation of the Hindu population. They condemned idolatry also as being the most fiercely attacked feature of Hinduism by the Muslims. The main feature of the movement was converting Muslims to Vedic Karma Kanda.

Then came the Ramakrishna Mission headed by Vivekananda. That movement was a further improvement upon the Arya Samaj. It did not discard avataratatva and idolatry as weeds. By that time Hinduism had gained enough strength to withstand the attacks by alien faiths on the important features of traditional Hinduism, that is, avataratva, Idol worship, yoga sastra, mantra sastra, etc. which it did not disown like the other earlier movements. Yet it did not identify completely with traditional Hinduism and passed stray dissenting opinions on some features of it. Varna based on birth was not so clearly accepted by them as by Gandhiji in Young India.

In the meantime the Theosophical Society manned by foreigners, professing Indian faiths, came into the religious arena of India. They were, in practice, at variance with the traditional Hindu religion: they were propagating some ultra-Hindu doctrines through their teachings. For instance, while Hinduism taught that varna based on birth related only to the body, Theosophy held that souls too had by nature some fixed varnas. However, these two movements were in their own way instrumental in stopping the rapid conversion of Hindu students to Christianity in South India.

From the time Gandhiji came into the arena, he augmented his political movements by his spiritual researches and devotion. Almost all the features of Hinduism that were discarded as weeds by the previous reform movements were clearly explained as being of indispensable utility. Even restrictions as regards marriage and dining among hereditary varnas were not disregarded by him. But his times were such that rules of untouchability laid down by our religion were being exploited by the British, the Christian missionaries and the Muslim politicals to serve their own selfish ends. It was in such an atmosphere that Gandhiji condemned it. Barring his views on untouchability, and a few such other points, his views on Ramanama, Ramayana, varna dharma, ahara niyama and the definition of God are such that the most faithful Hindu cannot but profit spiritually by digesting them.

The Parmacharya goes on to quote extensively and approvingly from Gandhiji's writings in Young India, the paper that Mahatma Gandhi ran from 1919 to 1932, on the fundamental principles of Sanatana dharma.

Mahatma Gandhi in his speeches and writings since early in his public life had repeatedly attempted to define the basic tenets of Sanatana dharma as he saw them. In a series of four lectures delivered in March 1905 at the Masonic Lodge in Johannesburg on the subject, Mahatma Gandhi assessed the contribution of the Brahmo Samaj, Arya Samaj and the Theosophical society he said in his speech:

> ...today we see few Hindus embracing Christianity in spite of the fact that the Christians are ruling over a vast kingdom. Nevertheless, Christianity has had a very considerable influence on Hinduism. Christian priests imparted education of a high order and pointed out some of the glaring defects in Hinduism, with the result that there arose among the Hindus other great teachers who, like Kabir, began to teach the Hindus what was good in Christianity and appealed to them to remove these defects. To this category belonged Raja Ram Mohan Rai, Devendra Nath Tagore and Keshab Chandra Sen. In Western India we had Dayanand Saraswati. And the numerous reform associations like the Brahmo Samaj and Arya Samaj that have sprung up in India today are doubtless the result of Christian influence. ...[6]

For his definition of the basic tenets of Sanatana dharma, we turn to a later article that he wrote following his visit to Madras presidency and other places in south India during the latter half of September 1921. It was during this visit to the heartland of Hindu orthodoxy, that Mahatma Gandhi took upon himself the further penance of wearing only a loincloth to cover his body. In a speech at Madurai on September 22, Mahatma Gandhi took the vow "to discard at least up to the 31st of October my topi and vest and to content myself with only a loincloth and a chaddar whenever found necessary for protection of my body."[7] The single loincloth became the regular dress of Mahatma Gandhi from then onwards, and thus he came to resemble even more a traditional Indian man of religion and divinity.

During this visit to south India, Mahatma Gandhi repeatedly asserted his claim of being a sanatani Hindu and perhaps meditated much on the meaning of being a follower of Sanatana dharma. Immediately following the visit, he wrote an article in the Young India of October 6 defining his conception of a sanatani Hindu. The definition he gave then surpasses his usual succinctness and simplicity of language. He wrote on his idea of sanatani Hindu:[8]

I call myself a sanatani Hindu, because,

1. I believe in the Vedas, the Upanishads, the Puranas and all that goes by the name of Hindu scriptures, and therefore in avataras and rebirth,
2. I believe in the varnashrama dharma in a sense in my opinion strictly Vedic but not in its present popular and crude sense,
3. I believe in the protection of the cow in its much larger sense than the popular,
4. I do not disbelieve in idol-worship.

It is this unqualified acceptance of the conceptual basis, the institutional framework and even the behavioural patterns of sanatana Hinduism that is at the core of Mahatma Gandhi's life and work. It is this acceptance which makes him and his thought perpetually relevant to India. And, since Sanatana dharma establishes the ideal form of man's relation with other created beings and with the universe as a whole, Mahatma Gandhi's thought remains relevant to all people of the world who seek to live in harmony amongst themselves and with the nature.

Having arisen from and been moulded by Sanatana dharma, Gandhiji's thought and work is all encompassing, it covers all aspects of life. In the following we shall take for detailed discussion a few facets which seem especially important today for the world, and particularly for India.

II The Gandhian Conception of *Swaraj*

Like all other aspects of life, the political and social organisation of society in India is supposed to be governed by the sanatana dharma. Society in the Indian conception is an organic formation composed of numerous groupings of people that emerge spontaneously around in a locality, a profession, a kinship community, or a religious faith. These groupings work according to the dharma that they inheres.. The king or the state in this conception is constituted to protect and preserve the dharma of these diverse groupings, and to guarantee the harmonious functioning of the organic groupings of the society according to their own inherent laws. The state does not lay down the law; it only protects the law, the dharma that is inherent in the society, existing as a unifying force.[9] It is the understanding of sanatana dharma that all aspects of creation have their inborn dharma, which provides harmonious existence and balance.. The state that preserves the inborn dharma in all organs of society is what is known as *Swaraj* in India.

Mahatma Gandhi while leading the struggle for independence from the British rule repeatedly emphasized the fact that his ultimate aim is not merely the overthrowing of alien rule, but the establishment of the conception of *Swaraj* in India. Even before arriving in India in the year 1915 to be a part of the national struggle for freedom, he wrote a small but seminal book by the name of Hind *Swaraj* to give a picture of his conception of *Swaraj* and the proposed means that is to be employed to achieve it.[10] Hind *Swaraj* was published in 1909 and ever since it has been reprinted several times.. Below, we shall have an occasion to refer to several of the precepts of this book. But, for giving a glimpse of Mahatma Gandhi's conception of *Swaraj*, we turn to the beautiful and evocative picture of his dreamed polity of "oceanic circles" that he drew in 1946, when independence for India was just around the corner. Offering a "broad but comprehensive picture of the Independent India of [his] own conception" for the benefit of the Congressmen who "in general certainly [did] not know the kind of independence they want," he wrote:[11]

Independence of India should mean independence of the whole of India... Independence must mean that of the people of India, not of those who are today ruling over them. The rulers should depend on the will of those who are under their heels. Thus, they have to be the servants of the people, ready to do their will.

Independence must begin at the bottom. Thus, every village will be a republic or panchayat having full powers. It follows, therefore, that every village has to be self-sustained and capable of managing its affairs even to the extent of defending itself against the whole world. It will be trained and prepared to perish in the attempt to defend itself against any onslaught from without. Thus, ultimately individual is the unit. This does not exclude dependence on and willing help from neighbours or from the world. It will be free and voluntary play of forces. Such a society is necessarily highly cultured in which every man and woman knows what he or she wants and, what is more, knows that no one should want anything that others cannot have with equal labour.

This society must naturally be based on truth and non-violence which, in my opinion, are not possible without a living belief in God, meaning a self-existent, all-knowing living Force which inheres every other force known to the world and which depends on none and which will live when all other forces may conceivably perish or cease to act. I am unable to account for my life without belief in this all-embracing living Light.

In this structure composed of innumerable villages, there will be ever-widening, never ascending circles. Life will not be a pyramid with the apex sustained by the bottom. But it will be an oceanic circle whose centre will be the individual always ready to perish for the village, the latter ready to perish for the circle of villages, till at last the whole becomes one life composed of individuals, never aggressive in their arrogance but ever humble, sharing the majesty of the oceanic circle of which they are integral units.

Therefore the outermost circumference will not wield power to crush the inner circle but will give strength to all within and derives its own strength from it. I may be taunted with the retort that this is all Utopian and, therefore, not worth a single thought. If Euclid's point, though incapable of being drawn by human agency, has an imperishable value, my picture has its own for mankind to live. Let India live for this true picture, though never realisable in its completeness. We must have a proper picture of what we want, before we can have something approaching it. If there ever is to be a republic of every village in India, then I claim verity for my picture in which the last is equal to the first or, in other words, no one is the first and none the last.

In this picture every religion has its full and equal place. We are all leaves of a majestic tree whose trunk cannot be shaken off its roots which are deep down in the bowels of the earth. The mightiest wind cannot move it.

Mahatma Gandhi was, as he admits, drawing a deliberately utopian picture of a society of selfless men deeply adhering to the *Sanatana* principle and seeing divine dignity and therefore equality in all creations. He wanted to place a highly evolved ideal thought before the soon to be independent India. Keenly looking at, his vision of an India composed of "the oceanic circles" consisting of an individual and his self-sustained locality (dharma) at the centre of the circle and expanding into ever widening circles to create larger and larger structures that draw their sustenance and legitimacy from the base of locality should not be considered as utopian. There is evidence to show that Indian polity before the arrival of the British was, in fact, based on locality-republics that coalesced to create and provide for the regional and other larger structures of the polity.

We can have the knowledge, in some detail, about the functioning of about 2000 localities in the late eighteenth century in a region around Madras in southern India. This region, referred to as the *Jaghire* in the early British records and later constituted into as the Chengalpattu district, was one of the first parts of the country to come under British rule. Before setting up new administrative arrangements in the area, the British tried to investigate the administrative structures that had already existed there. The investigations involved an intensive survey of all aspects of life covering almost all localities of the region. The records of the survey, which was conducted between 1767 to 1774, are available both in the original Tamil accounts written on palm-leafs and in the English summaries, prepared for the British administrators in India and their principals in London.[12]

The polity described in these records is indeed like the "oceanic circles" the polity conceived by Mahatma Gandhi. The localities of the region functioned like autonomous republics that budgeted and provided for the administrative, military, economic, cultural and educational services of the locality and also for the larger polity of the region around it.

The main instrument of political and economic organisation in these localities comprised of an elaborate system of allocating shares of the produce of the locality to a variety of functions and beneficiaries. The survey records list about a hundred distinct services and institutions for which the shares were taken out from the produce of different localities of the region, and on an average each of the localities took out shares for about thirty of these. The beneficiaries of such shares were including cultural institutions and functionaries like temples, mathams and chatrams, scholars and teachers, musicians and dancers, also including economic services like irrigation and measurement of corn, and the administrative services like registry and militia. Some of these institutions and services were entirely local: for example the village temple, or the barber and washerman who functioned for and received shares from a single locality or at the most from the neighbouring group of two or three localities. Others like the great temples, the high scholars, the regional registrars, and more importantly the militia leaders functioned at a level that extended far beyond the locality. Several of these regional institutions and functionaries received shares from hundreds of localities in the region.

The shares that the various institutions and functionaries received were not nominal. On the average about 30 percent of the produce of a locality had given for such sharing. The shares of different services and institutions were given for providing proper maintenance and upkeep. The arrangement was in fact similar to the budgeting mechanism of a state, because through such sharing the locality allocated resources for different functions essential to a particular locality, as well as provided for the larger polity of the region surrounding it. The locality within itself was thus indeed function as the state that arranged and provided for its internal cultural, political, economic and administrative functions. And, at levels of polity beyond itself, the locality was not only the basic constituent unit, but also the constituting authority. By setting aside shares for the trans-locality institutions and services, the localities in a region together provided for and created with it the larger levels of the polity. This was the nature of the polity that had being functioning in India from times immemorial until the British administration. Mahatma Gandhi while presenting his vision of the "oceanic circles" polity in 1946 on the eve of independence was only reminding the Indiana of her own administrative practices before the British rule..

The case of study of Chengalpattu localities reveals certain salient feature of sharing. Besides the allocation of the shares from the produce of the land, the Chengalpattu localities also practiced another kind of sharing. This consisted in assignment of revenue from parts of the cultivated lands to essentially the same set of institutions and services that had received shares of the produce. Such assignments are called *manyams*, which were very common. Almost a quarter of the cultivated lands in the region were classified as *manyam* lands. But, since about one-third of the produce of a locality was already taken out as shares of different institutions and functionaries, the fraction of the produce that the lands paid as revenue could not have been very significant. And therefore, unlike the share in the produce, this share in the revenue was probably of no great economic value to the recipient.

The *manyam* constitution, it seems, were constituted to give effect to another important aspect of the polity. To have a share in the right to receive revenue is to share in sovereignty; and sharing of the sovereignty amongst many is a cherished ideal of the classical Indian polity based on Sanatana dharma. These arrangements of sharing the produce and the revenue in the Chengalpattu polity covered all institutions and all households, except those of the direct producers of wealth - the cultivators, the traders and the weavers. The producers of wealth, and especially the cultivators, of course, provided for themselves and for all others, and thus were sovereign of their own.

Such wide dispersal of sovereignty is natural and essential in a polity constructed on the principle of organic units and groupings functioning according to their inherent dharma. In such a polity every individual, every household, every locality and every other grouping of the people partakes the sovereignty. Every household and grouping has the sovereign right to decide what is right and what is wrong according to its own inherent laws. From this right to discriminate between right and wrong follows the duty to refuse the commandments that are perceived to be wrong, are against the dharma of the group or household concerned - a duty from which Mahatma Gandhi derived his concept of *satyagraha*.

III How the Concept of *Satyagraha* Conceived

The duty and the right of every constituent unit (locality) of the society to defend its dharma against illegitimate commandments of even a legitimate king or a state is what Mahatma Gandhi called variously as passive resistance, civil disobedience or *Satyagraha* (meaning the insistence on truth). These were the celebrated instruments of political self-assertion that Mahatma Gandhi perfected during his experiments to fight authority in South Africa, and he effectively used it to awaken the Indian people that lead them to independence. However, we should be aware of the fact Mahatma Gandhi did not invent these concepts. These followed directly from the conception of *Swaraj* founded on the principles of *Sanatana* dharma that India had always cherished and practiced.

Mahatma Gandhi identified and insisted that India has always been a nation of passive resisters and that "the nation at large has generally used passive resistance in all departments of life." Defining the concept of passive resistance, for which he used the term *satyagraha* in the original Gujarati, in Hind *Swaraj*, he wrote:[13]

> The real meaning of the statement that we are a law-abiding nation is that we are passive resisters. When we do not like certain laws, we do not break the heads of the law-givers but we suffer and do not submit to the laws. That we should obey laws whether good or bad is a new-fangled notion. There was no such thing in the former days. The people disregarded those laws they did not like and suffered the penalties for their breach. It is contrary to our manhood if we obey laws repugnant to our conscience. Such teaching is opposed to religion and means slavery. If the Government to ask us to go without any clothing, should we do so? If I were a passive resister, I would say to them that I would have nothing to do with their law. But we have so forgotten ourselves and become so compliant that we do not mind any degrading law [....].
>
> The fact is that, in India, the nation at large has generally used passive resistance in all departments of life. We cease to co-operate with our rulers when they displease us. This is passive resistance.
>
> I remember an instance when, in a small principality, the villagers were offended by some command issued by the prince. The former immediately began vacating the village. The prince became nervous, apologised to his subjects and withdrew the command. Many such instances can be found in India. Real Home Rule is possible only where passive resistance is the guiding force of the people. Any other rule is foreign rule.

Classical Indian texts of polity recommend even stronger means than passive resistance against kings who deviate from dharma. The Mahabharata, in an oft-quoted passage defining the duties of the people against a delinquent king, says:

> A king who does not protect the people, who imposes oppressive exactions upon them, who extinguishes the opportunities of livelihood, and who does not lead, such a king is indeed kali. The people should surround and kill such a cruel king. Having given his promise to protect the people, a king who does not protect, he indeed should be killed by the people as a sick and mad dog.[14]

No wonder that the early British scholars were surprised to notice that the kings in India often seemed to be afraid of their subjects.[15] The kind of strong measures recommended in the above passage of the Mahabharata might been probably rarely employed in those days. But passive resistance, it seems, remained part of the day-to-day political functioning of the country, at least, up to early nineteenth century. It was normal for the people to refuse to obey commands that they perceived to be against the customs and practices, to organise collective public demonstrations of their unhappiness with such rules , and, ultimately, to collectively quit the principality where such commandments prevailed.

Mahatma Gandhi in the passage from Hind *Swaraj*, quoted above, mentions an instance of passive resistance from his personal knowledge. There are records of many such instances that continued to occur sporadically throughout the nineteenth century. There is a particularly well-documented instance of a rather intense civil disobedience instance that began in the city of Varanasi in the present state of Uttar Pradesh and spread to several towns in Bihar and West Bengal during 1801-11.[16]

The events were concerned with the institution of a tax on houses by the British East India Company. The tax was enacted through Regulation XV of October 6, 1810. The first steps to promulgate with the implementation of the Regulation in Varanasi were initiated in the middle of December. By December 25, the Acting Magistrate at Varanasi had reported that "a very serious situation has been excited among all ranks and descriptions of the city by the promulgation of Regulation XV, 1810. [······] The people are extremely clamorous; they have shut up their shops, abandoned their usual occupations, and assembled in multitudes with a view to extort from me an immediate compliance with their demands.[······]" On December 28; the Acting Magistrate was addressing another communication to the Government conveying the urgency of the situation and emphasising the generality and determination of the protest:[17]

> [······] An oath was administered throughout the city, both among the Hindoos and the Mahommedans, enjoining all classes to neglect their respective occupations until I should consent to direct the Collector to remove the assessors and give a positive assurance that the tax should be abolished. It was expected that the outcry and distress occasioned by this general conspiracy would extort from me the concessions they required. The Lohars, the Mistrees, the Jolahirs, the Hujams, the Druzees, the Kahars, the Bearers, every class of workmen engaged unanimously in this conspiracy, and it was carried to such an extent that on the 26th, the dead bodies were actually cast neglected into the Ganges, because the proper people could not be prevailed upon to administer the customary rites. These several classes of people, attended by multitudes of other ranks and descriptions have collected at a place in the vicinity of the city, from whence they declare nothing but force shall remove them, unless I consent to yield the point for which they are contending.

The protest continued for about two months, during which thousands of people remained assembled in the open fields, exposing themselves to the harsh north-Indian winter. At the end they withdrew to their houses with a sullen indifference towards an authority that did not understand the time-honoured rules of engagements and interactions between the rulers and the people. The people of Varanasi repeatedly tried to make the British administrators to be aware of these rules. In the final petition they addressed to the Governor-General of the British East India Company on February 7, 1811, they especially emphasised that their protest was in consonance with the "manner and custom in this country from time immemorial" and that such protest in no way constituted a "disturbance," as the British administrators tended to describe it. Their formulation in this context needs to be quoted in full:[18]

> As a number of persons continued for some time assembled together to complain, Government conceived that there was disturbance, and so it was declared in the proclamation of the 13th of January, 1811. Sire, if an order be passed relating particularly to one individual, and other persons combine to support him, it might in that case be denominated a disturbance. As the introduction of the tax affected every individual of every class, every one presented himself to obtain justice. Thousands of men and women, all the old and infirm, Brahmins, devotees and Pundits, who have no occupation but prayer and penance, abandoned their houses and were among them. None were armed, even with a stick. The manner and custom in this country from time immemorial is this: that, whenever any act affecting every one generally is committed by the Government, the poor, the aged, the infirm, the women all forsake their families and their homes, expose themselves to the inclemency of the seasons and to other kinds of inconveniences, and make known their affliction and distress, that the Government, which is more considerate than our parents, may observe their condition and extend indulgences to its subjects. Besides this, when the Brahmins in general are involved in distress, it is incumbent on all Hindoos to abstain from receiving sustenance, and anyone who presumes to deviate from this custom must incur general opprobrium. If your petitioners, by assembling together in this manner, can be considered to have created a disturbance, it is our misfortune.

The people also insisted that their objection to the tax was not so much against the economic burden imposed by the tax, but against the nature of the tax. They were agitated because they believed that a tax on houses was against the customary law, against dharma as it was, and an encroachment upon their sovereign privileges. In the petition of February 7, 1811, they wrote:[19]

> ...... in the Shera and Sahster, together with the customs of Hindostan ...... houses are reckoned one of the principal necessaries of life, and are not accounted disposable property. Even creditors cannot claim them from us in satisfaction of their dues; and in this country, in the times of Mohamedan and Hindoo princes, houses were never rendered liable to contribution for the service of the state... hence it is that under the English Government, in the sale of estates to realise the public revenue, the houses of landholders are exempted.

By this time the British authorities had begun to form some appreciation of the sentiments of the people. The Acting Magistrate in his letter forwarding the final petition of the people to the Government wrote:[20]

> ...... I feel it my duty, however, to state generally for the information of the Government, what I believe to be the real sentiments of the people. I believe the objection which they entertain against the measure in question is pointed exclusively at the nature and principle of the tax, and not in the least at the rate of assessment by which it will be realised. The inhabitants of this city appear to consider it an innovation, which, according to the laws and usages of the country, they imagine no government has the right to introduce; and that unless they protest against, the tax will be speedily increased, and the principle of it extended so as to affect everything which they call their own. Under the circumstances, I fear, they will not easily reconcile themselves to the measure. To declare the assessment permanently limited to the rate established by the Regulation, would of course be satisfactory to them; yet the general repugnance is to the tax itself, and while the inhabitants at large profess themselves disposed to submit to any tax, however, oppressive, if established according to the usage of

> the country, they appear to think it a hardship to be compelled to contribute a sum, however inconsiderable, in any mode to which they are unaccustomed.

Heitle, a historian of these events, comes to the conclusion that the house-tax was not only perceived as an innovation inconsistent with the custom and usage of the country, it was also seen as an encroachment into the autonomous domain of what he calls the mohalla (urban locality) Government. The mohalla Government, and other locality and caste level organisations of the people, especially the caste panchayats were actively involved in the organisation of the protest. According to an observer of the time, the protest gathering was not a disorderly mob, but a highly organised assembly functioning under the government, as it were, of the diverse inborn organic units of the society, especially the caste *panchayats*:[21]

> Instead of appearing like a tumultuous and disorderly mob, the vast multitudes came forth in a state of perfect organisation: each caste trade and profession occupied a distinct spot on the ground, and was regulated in all its acts by the orders of its own panchayat, who invariably punished all instances of misconduct or disobedience on the part of its members. The state of things continued for more than a month; and whilst the authority of the British Government was, in a manner, suspended, the influence of the panchayat was sufficient to maintain great order and tranquility.

The protest was, thus, not merely a conflict between the people and their rulers, but between state-like organs of the society that were sovereign within their own domains and an alien government that waged claim of exclusive sovereignty in all domains and extinguished all other sovereignties.

We have recounted these events at some length, because they illustrate almost all aspects of the Indian concept of *swaraj*, constituted of organic groupings of the people functioning according to their own inherent dharma, and partaking of the sovereignty that always remains widely dispersed in the society. The events also graphically illustrate the Indian insistence on the right and duty to offer resistance when some organ of the society attempts to violate the dharma, or encroach upon the sovereignty of others dharma, and, thus, threaten the ideals of *swaraj*. The events are particularly important for showing in such detail and intensity that both the concept and practice of *swaraj* and *satyagraha* had remained vibrantly alive amongst the Indian people even as late as the beginning of the nineteenth century.

Perhaps the most important aspect of Mahatma Gandhi's thought and work is in reviving the memory of *swaraj* and *satyagraha* amongst the Indian people, and giving them the courage and organisational strength to begin practicing these timeless concepts of Indian polity once again. This also is the aspect of Mahatma Gandhi's thought and work that remains greatly relevant for India as well as the rest of the world even today.

During the fifty years since Mahatma Gandhi's departure from this world, the strength and reach of centralised bureaucracies and markets has been increasing everywhere enormously. With the rapid improvement and spread of the technologies of communication and the gathering of information, these centralising institutions today are in a position to intervene and direct almost all aspects of an individual's life. In spite of the ritual obeisance being paid to the concept of individual liberty, the individual today is forced to surrender his discriminations and choices, his sense of right and wrong, etc. to the centralising and faceless systems. And the natural groupings and communities that form the bedrock of an individual's freedom of discrimination and action are losing all relevance. In this atmosphere individuals and their communities all over the world are, more and more, requiring to need the concepts of *swaraj* and *satyagraha* to retain and win back some space for the exercise of their sovereign discrimination and autonomous functioning.

This aspect of Mahatma Gandhi's thought and work is even more relevant for India today. Though India won her freedom from the British rule by performing large-scale *satyagraha* for achieving *swaraj*, yet the state that India created after independence had little in common with the ideal of *swaraj*. It is an irony of history that an independence struggle fought under the leadership of Mahatma Gandhi for the re-establishment of the Indian ideals of *swaraj*, resulted in a constituent assembly that took it to be its task to create a constitution that would eliminate all traces of the traditional Indian ways of functioning from the public life of India. The constituent assembly, therefore, chose to retain the colonial structures that centralised all discrimination and initiative in the alien institutions of bureaucracy and judiciary, and left no space for the organic groupings of the society.

In India the localities and communities that traditionally shared in sovereignty and formed the basic constituent units of *swaraj* were more thoroughly emasculated than in almost any other part of the world. Because, for the colonial administration, the establishment of sovereignty over India meant mainly in subduing, disbanding and dispersing these constituent units, that claimed shares in sovereignty.

But local and community level groupings of people, even when not endowed with sovereignty as they were existed in India prior to the British rule, are essential for the smooth and effective functioning of any society. Centralised bureaucracies may boast of great discrimination, foresight and authority, but they, generally, are unable to deliver much at the ground level without the initiative and participation of the local communities. Since in India the localities and communities have been so thoroughly emasculated, Indian society at the ground level seems to have lost all its initiatives. Mahatma Gandhi's ideas of *swaraj* and *satyagraha*; therefore, remain as urgently relevant to India today as they were in 1915 when he arrived in India to help regain the dignity and freedom.

When India recovers her ideal of *swaraj* and begins to function once again according to the principles that it has been following for ages and that Mahatma Gandhi revived it so recently, India shall present an example that the modern world may profitably emulate to remove and free itself of the dehumanising yoke of centralising bureaucracies and consumer culture. This is why Mahatma Gandhi had always believed that freedom for India would open the path of freedom for the world.

IV Gandhian ideal State, *Ramarajya*

In Gandhi Smriti, Birla House, New Delhi and at several other places associated with the memory of Mahatma Gandhi, there displayed a talisman given by Gandhiji to his countrymen, reading:

> I will give you a talisman. Whenever you are in doubt or when the self becomes too much with you, apply the following test:
>
> Recall the face of the poorest and the weakest man whom you have seen and ask yourself if the step you contemplate is going to be of any use to him. Will he gain anything by it? Will it restore him to control over his own life and destiny? In other words, will it lead to Swaraj for the hungry and spiritually starving millions?
>
> Then you will find your doubts and yourself melting away.

This striving to care for the last one, to create a political system that would take into account and provide for "the poorest and the weakest formed the focal point of Mahatma Gandhi's thought and action. He returns to it again and again, where he is willing to sacrifice almost everything else for achieving this one aim. *Swaraj* for him meant nothing; if it could not ensure that everyone unto the last one is fed, clothed and housed with dignity. And the first task of independent India for him was to provide quickly for the dignified fulfillment of the basic needs of everyone. Speaking to students from Santiniketan in April 7, 1947, before the departure of the British from India, he said to the students:[22]

> In the end I would only say that under swarajya, efforts should be made for providing everyone at least with a square meal, enough clothing to cover himself and a house to live in. At present while some have utensils of gold and silver, others have not

even pots of clay - some have garments of silk and brocade whereas others have not even enough clothing to cover their nakedness.

Mahatma Gandhi at that time was staying in a Bhangi colony, a habitation of scavengers. Gandhi, towards the latter part of his life preferred more and more to live amongst the poorest and the lowest class of people. His insistence on caring for the deprived and the depressed was in some ways similar to the ideas of Tolstoy and Ruskin, and in general to the socialist ideals. But for him such caring to the needy was also part of the Indian tradition; it was the essence of Ramarajya, the reign of the ideal king, The reign of Sri Rama, which defines the ideal good times for the Indians. In fact Ramarajya was dharmarajya, the reign based on the precepts of sanatana dharma.

In the Gandhian conception *swarajya*, *dharmarajya* and *Ramarajya* were synonymous denoting the tenets of sanatana dharma. He used the three terms interchangeably, and the essence of all three for him was in securing peace and enough for all, that includes the last person. Thus in 1936 we hear him saying that respect may be given to the Maharaja of Mysore to approach more and more to Ramarajya in Mysore which implicitly emphasis that "in olden days, Ramarajya meant a government in which everyone in the country, including the lowest ryot, had peace and plenty."[23]

In defining Ramarajya as the era of peace and plenty for all, Mahatma Gandhi was closely following the classical Indian understanding. In the Ramayana of Valmiki, the epic narrating the story of Sri Rama, Ramarajya is described as the age when:

> There is happiness and cheer all around. All are contented. All are well-nourished. All follow dharma. All are in good health. All are without disease. And, all are free from fear and hunger.[1]

And to ensure that all partake of such plenty and peace, the king is enjoined to take special care of the poor and the weak. In this context the Mahabharata advises the king in these words:

> Always arrange for the welfare and the livelihood of those who have no resources, those who have no one to look after them, those who are afflicted by old age, and those who have lost their husbands.[25]

> Wiping away tears from the faces of the destitute, the orphans and the old, and spreading cheer amongst all - this is known as the dharma of the king.[26]

Taking care of the destitute and the weak, the king in fact becomes "the strength of the weak and the orphaned, the eyes of those who cannot see and the legs of those who cannot walk."[27] This is the nature of Ramarajya that Mahatma Gandhi wanted to revive.

Mahatma Gandhi calling upon India to cherish and revive the tradition of caring for all and ensuring dignified plenty and peace for even the poorest and weakest, , he repeatedly emphasised two further aspects of the Indian understanding of Ramarajya. First, that taking care of the poorest and the weakest was not the responsibility of the king alone, but all resourceful and wealthy people in the society needed to share in to this responsibility. In the verses quoted above and elsewhere in classical Indian literature, references to the king in such contexts obviously include all, all responsible householders (*grahasthas*). Secondly, such caring for the Indians was not a matter of charity or personal benevolence; it was a matter of one's own dharma,. In an article in the Navajivan,March 22, 1931, Gandhi offered a particularly succinct exposition of these two aspects of his conception of Ramarajya.[28]

Satyagraha is understood to be an attempt to make the possible a reality . Truth implies justice. A just administration implies an era of truth and justice, or *swaraj*, *dharmarajya*, *Ramarajya* or in other words in modern parlance the people's raj (democracy). In such a government the ruler would be the protector and friend of the subjects that he rules. Between the way of life of the ruler and that of the poorest of his subjects, there should not be a huge gap that is there today. There would be an appropriate similarity between the king's palace and the huts of the subjects. Such that the difference between the needs of the two would be a little; both would enjoy pure air and water. They should have sufficient food to eat. The ruler would give up eating fifty-six different kinds of delicacies and be satisfied with only six. If the poor use utensils made of wood or mud, the ruler may well use utensils made of such metals as brass. On the other hand, the ruler who wants to use utensils of gold and silver must be robbing his subjects. The poor should be able to obtain sufficient clothing according to his style of living. Let the king have more clothes, but let the difference be not such as to cause envy. The children of both should be studying in the same primary school. The ruler should act like a senior member of the family of the poor. If he does anything for the good of the poor, he should not regard it as a favour that he has conferred upon them. Benevolence has no place in dharma. It is the dharma of the ruler to serve and take care of his subjects. What has been said in regard to the ruler applies to all wealthy persons; likewise it is the dharma of the poor not to bear malice towards the rich.

Early British records indicate that the kings of India indeed followed the ideals of dharma desired by Mahatma Gandhi. They maintained a lifestyle similar to that of their subjects; their personal expenses were often very limited , while they spent liberally on feeding and caring for the poor and needy.[29] However, what is of particular relevance for our present discussion is Gandhiji's assertion that such caring for the subjects arose not from benevolence, but from *dharma*.

According to the Indian perspective, the universe is a great cycle of give and take (dependence) between different aspects of creation. Whatever is earned or produced by man is in fact taken from the share of other aspects of creation and it may rightfully be consumed only after returning the shares to all, meaning only after propitiating and fulfilling all other parts of creation. Consuming without having propitiated others is indeed considered as stealing. Brahman, the creator, while initiating this great cycle of the universe enjoins upon human beings to keep it moving through *yajna*, which can be explained as the disciplined action that propitiates and fulfils all aspects of creation. The one who does not keep this cycle of mutual dependence - the dharma chakra, as it is often referred to - moving is a sinner immersed merely in the pleasures of senses. The life of such a living being is a waste.

The imperative of caring and providing for the poor and the weak is derived from this essential understanding of the universe. The foregoing paragraph is a free paraphrase of verses 10-16 of the third chapter of the Bhagavad Gita, . All classical Indian literatures, the Vedas, the Upanishads, the Itihasas and the Puranas, present the same understanding of the universe in diverse ways and forms.[30] The Gita's exposition is however probably the simplest. It is therefore not surprising that Mahatma Gandhi used it persistently to his listeners, and especially young students, to these verses of the Gita. Particularly during his visit to south India in August-September 1927, he took these verses of the Gita as the text of his speeches. During this visit, he spoke in several cities and towns, and almost everywhere he referred to these verses as forming the core of the Gita. Below, we quote from a speech he gave to the students of the Hindu High School at Madras on September 4, 1927.[31]

> Those of you who know Sanskrit should tomorrow, if possible today, buy the Gita - and I understand you can get the book for a very small price - and begin to study the book. Have private Gita classes for yourselves. Those of you who do not know Sanskrit should study Sanskrit only for the sake of the Gita. If you have not got that much facility, then you should read Gita written in English or Tamil, if there is a Tamil translation of it. I tell you that it contains treasures of knowledge of which you have no conception whatsoever. I suggest to you that at first you may begin to read the third chapter of the Gita. You will find there the gospel of selfless work expounded in a most convincing manner. Selfless work there is described characteristically by one beautiful word called yajna. If you will read the book with my eyes you will find charkha also described there. There is

one passage which says that "He who eats without serving, without yajna, is a thief (III.12)."

The association of charkha, the spinning wheel, with the wheel of creation, with the great cycle of mutual give and take (dependence) is described in these verses of the Gita and it is indeed interesting in the Gandhian context. Gandhiji believed that charkha by empowering the poorest and the weakest of the Indians would restore the reign of dharma, and also would set the cycle of give and take moving again.

The essential understanding of the term *Ramarajya* that Mahatma Gandhi envisaged to re-establish in India was based on such fundamental understanding of the universe and of the relations between its different aspects that exists in such a universe. In this understanding, which is also the foundation of *sanatana* dharma, all have a share in the totality of the created, and all have a responsibility to ensure that no part of the creation is deprived of with its proper share. *Apastamaba Dharmasutra* puts it: [33]"no one is forced to suffer from hunger and disease, or from the extremes of heat and cold,"

Mahatma Gandhi saw in the Indian veneration for the cow as a symbolic acceptance of this *sanatana* dharma requirement to care and provide for all the creation. In the article on the discipline of a *sanatani* Hindu that we have quoted in the first section, he explained the position of the cow in Hinduism thus: [34]

> The central fact of Hinduism however is cow-protection. Cow-protection to me is one of the most wonderful phenomena in human evolution. It takes the human being beyond his species. The cow to me means the entire sub-human world. Man through the cow is enjoined to realise his identity with all that lives. Why the cow was selected for apotheosis is obvious to me. The cow was in India the best companion. She was the giver of plenty. Not only did she give milk, but she also made agriculture possible. The cow is a poem of pity. One reads pity in the gentle animal. She is a mother to millions of Indian mankind. Protection of the

cow means protection of the whole dumb creation of God. The ancient seer, whoever he was, began with the cow. The appeal of the lower order of creation is all the more forcible because it is speechless. Cow-protection is the gift of Hinduism to the world. And Hinduism will live so long as there are Hindus to protect the cow.

The establishment of *Rmarajya* or *Dharmarajya*, where all are provided for and all receive their proper share in the universe remains an unfulfilled dream. In the world of today, there are a large number of human beings who have to go without sufficient food and clothing, and a roof over their heads. Even in the wealthy parts of the world many are forced to roam the streets, begging for food and live without proper shelter but often fail to receive anything properly. According to the Indian understanding such a situation is intolerable. This is the situation of *yugakshaya*, the end of times. It happens only when the current cycle of creation is about to end, when the world has moved far away from the ideals of *Ramarajya* (*sanatana* dharma), that "people are reduced to the selling of food," and even "those who seek arc rcfuscd food, water and shelter and are thus seen lying around on the roads."[35]

The situation of India in this regard is perhaps worse than that of most other countries of the world. A considerable number of the Indian people today fail to get two square meals a day, a majority of the Indian children are malnourished, a preponderant majority of the pregnant women are anaemic. The availability of food per person in India today is such that for many people death from starvation is barely kept off the door. The situation is almost equally bad in the matter of water, clothing and shelter.

Where men are barely fed than animals, they can hardly fair better. In the land that proudly made the humble cow the symbol of her civilisation, and serving the cow a fundamental precept of her religion, today, there is little food available for the animals. As the men and children, so do the cows and calves, roam the streets of India in a state of hunger, thirst and sickness.

India has not followed the discipline of caring and providing for all that the *sanatana dharma* teaches and that Mahatma Gandhi sought to revive with the independence. India in fifty years of her independence has not been able to take the first step towards *Ramarajya*, that of ensuring an availability of sufficient food for all. This aspect of Mahatma Gandhi's thought and work therefore remains urgently relevant.

India needs to recall the *santatana* dharma doctrine that Mahatma Gandhi gave, begin thinking once again of the poorest and the weakest, and begin organising her polity and economy so as to fulfill the basic needs of food, clothing and shelter for all. India gave the concept of *Ramarajya* to the world. It is primarily the responsibility of India to begin realising the meaning of *Ramarajya*. But the conception of *Ramarajya* is relevant for the whole world. When India reverts to the discipline and begins establishing *Ramarajya* for the people, it shall once again be able to teach the world that peace and plenty for all is the fundamental condition of existence, and that the hunger of even one human being or any other creature destroys the universal dharma. . Therefore, if the world is to exist the ideals of *Ramarajya*.must be respected. Mahatma Gandhi certainly believed so.

V. Gandhian Apprehensions Concerning Technology

Discussing the questions concerning technology and machinery in Hind *Swaraj*, the little yet exhaustive book that he wrote early in his life, in 1910, and that presents perhaps the most authentic and precise exposition of Mahatma Gandhi's way of thinking, Mahatma Gandhi wrote:[36]

> It is machinery that has impoverished India. It is difficult to measure the harm that Manchester has done to us. It is because of Manchester that Indian handicraft has all but disappeared.
>
> Machinery has begun to desolate Europe. Ruination is now knocking at the English gates. Machinery is the chief symbol of modern civilisation; it represents a great sin.

> The workers in the mills of Bombay have become slaves. The condition of the women working in the mills is shocking. When there were no mills, these women were not starving. If the machinery craze grows in our country, it will become an unhappy land. It may be considered a heresy, but I am bound to say that it were better for us to send money to Manchester and to use flimsy Manchester cloth then to multiply mills in India. By using Manchester cloth we only waste our money; but by reproducing Manchester in India, we shall keep our money at the price of our blood, because our very moral being will be sapped, and I call in support of my statement the very mill-hands as witnesses.

Writing about the railways, the Mahatma used even stronger language:[37]

> It must manifest to you that, but for the railways, the English could not have such a hold on India as they have. The railways, too, have spread the bubonic plague. Without them the masses could not move from place to place. They are the carriers of plague germs. Formerly, we had natural segregation. Railways have also increased the frequency of famines because, owing to facility of means of locomotion, people sell out their grain and it is sent to the dearest markets. People become careless and so the pressure of famine increases. Railways accentuate the evil nature of man. Bad men fulfil their evil designs with greater rapidity. The holy places of India have become unholy. Formerly, people went to these places with very great difficulty. Generally, therefore, only the real devotees visited such places. Nowadays rogues visit them to practice their roguery.
>
> Good travels at a snail's pace - it can, therefore, have little to do with the railways. Those who want to do good are not selfish, they are not in a hurry, they know that to impregnate people with good requires a long time. But evil has wings. To build a house takes time. Its destruction takes none. So the railways can become a distributing agency for the evil one only. It may be a debatable matter whether railways spread famines, but it is beyond dispute that they propagate evil.

In the early parts of the twentieth century, the disruption of social and economic life of India was caused by the large scale imports of machine made goods from Britain, especially the mill-made cloth, and the spread of railways could be seen all around India. Such disruption and dislocation had begun when the British acquired control of several parts of India in the latter half of eighteenth century. The process was however highly accelerated with the arrival of Railways in the 1850's and consequent opening of the domestic markets to the imported goods. The visible and widespread disruption and destitution of India was probably what gave a bitter edge to Mahatma Gandhi's rejection of the industrial scale machinery and technology.

Mahatma Gandhi construed his rejection of imported products of industrial machinery into a means of the awakening and emancipation of India. The *swadeshi* movement, involving boycott imported machine-made goods became a movement of both as a political protest and a tool for the economic reconstruction of India.

Mahatma Gandhi's views on technology and machinery, thus, had a basis in the political and economic conditions of India. But his rejection of technology and machinery went far beyond the immediate situation of India. It was, as we shall see shortly, anchored much deeper, in the essential understanding of the universe and man's role and place in it as enshrined in the *sanatana dharma*. That is why in the passages quoted above, we hear him invoking terms like 'great sin,' 'evil' and 'unholy,' while referring to machinery and railways. At another place in Hind *Swaraj*, he formulated the argument in explicitly ethical terms:[38]

> The more we indulge our passions the more unbridled they become. Our ancestors, therefore, set a limit to our indulgences. ...... It was not that we did not know how to invent machinery, but our forefathers knew that, if we set our hearts after such things, we would become slaves and lose our moral fibre. They, therefore, after due deliberation decided that we should only do what we could with our hands and feet. ...... They saw that

> kings and their swords were inferior to the sword of ethics, and they, therefore, held the sovereigns of the earth to be inferior to the Rishis and the Fakirs. A nation with a constitution like that is fitter to teach others than to learn from others. This nation had courts, lawyers and doctors, but they were all within bounds. Everybody knew that these professions were not particularly superior; moreover, these vakils and vaids did not rob people; they were considered people's dependents, not their masters. ......

All civilisations barring the modern-Western civilisation have harboured such ambivalence about technology and machinery, as well as about the men of 'technological' professions. They have worried that complex mechanical contraptions might make man go against the rule of nature, and might carry away man from the right path and move him towards evil and ruin. Joseph Needham, the modern historian of classical Chinese science and society, quotes, in this context, a passage from a third century B.C. Chinese text of Chuang Tzu. The passage, a representative of similar passages found in several other Chinese texts of diverse periods, reads: [39]

> Tzu-Kung had been wandering in the south in Chhu, and was returning to Chin. As he passed a place north of the Han (river), he saw an old man working in a garden. Having dug his channels, he kept on going down into a well, and returning with water in a large jar. This caused him much expenditure of strength for very small results. Tzu-Kung said to him, 'There is a contrivance (chieh) by mans of which a hundred plots of ground may be irrigated in one day. Little effort will accomplish much. Would you, Sir, not like to try it?' The farmer looked up at him and said, 'How does it work?' Tzu-Kung said, 'It is a lever made of wood, heavy behind and light in front. It raises water quickly so that it comes flowing into a ditch gurgling in a steady foaming stream. Its name is the swape (kao).' The farmer's face suddenly changed and he laughed, 'I have heard from my master,' he said 'that those who have cunning devices use cunning in their affairs, and that those who use cunning in their affairs have

> cunning hearts. Such cunning means the loss of pure simplicity. Such a loss leads to restlessness of the spirit, and with such men the Tao will not dwell. I knew all about (the swape), but I would be ashamed to use it.'

The ancient civilisations, contrary to the modern-West were ambivalent not just about technological contraptions, but they harboured similar reservations about what may be called the 'technical' knowledge; the knowledge that seeks to look behind things, to lay bare nature and its workings, as it naturally functions. Needham, in the context quoted above, collects several instances of such ambivalence from the Chinese texts. We shall, however, quote a parable of Hosso Buddhism narrated by Yukio Mishima in his Spring Snow. In the novel it is attributed to the Abbess of the Gesshu Temple on the outskirts of Nara:[40]

> You remember the story is set in Tang China. A man named Yuan Hsaio was on his way to the famous Mount Kaoyu to study the teaching of Buddha. When night fell, he happened to be beside a cemetery, so he lay down to sleep among the burial mounds. Then in the middle of the night he awoke with a terrible thirst. Stretching out his hand, he scooped up some water from a hole by his side. As he dozed off again, he thought to himself that never had water tasted so pure, so fresh and cold. But when morning came, he saw what he had drunk from in the dark. Incredible though it seemed, what had tasted so delicious was water that had collected in a human skull. He retched and was sick. Yet this experience taught something to Yuan Hsaio. He realised that as long as conscious desire is at work, it will permit distinctions to exist. But if one can suppress it, these distincions dissolve and one can be as content with a skull as with anything else.
>
> But what interests me is this: once Yuan Hsaio had been thus enlightened, could he drink that water again, secure in the knowledge that it was pure and delicious? ……

The last comment is not by the Abbess, but by a person called Honda, the rationalistic friend of the protagonist of the novel. The Abbess of the Gesshu Temple tells the parable to introduce her listeners to the doctrine of Yuishiki, the doctrine that all existence is based on subjective awareness. But it also is a parable of the ambivalence about knowledge that goes behind the visible reality that reveals the inner working of nature. And that is how Yukio Mishima seems to read it.

The Panchatantra, the Indian treasure-book of moral stories tells a similar story that counterpoises vidya, knowledge of the *sastras*, systemized knowledge against *buddhi*, the discriminating intellect, the intellect that differentiates between right and wrong. The parable reads thus:[41]

> Once upon a time, there lived, in a city, four Brahmin boys. They were all close friends. Three of them were highly learned in the sastras, but had little discrimination. The fourth was well endowed with buddhi, the discriminating intellect, but had no interest in the sastras.
>
> Once, the four of them decided thus, 'What use is learning, *vidya*, if it is not employed to earn riches by travelling to foreign lands and gratifying the kings? Let us therefore travel to the eastern countries to seek wealth.'
>
> Having decided thus, they set out on their journey. When they had gone some distance, the eldest said, 'Look, the fourth amongst us lacks learning. He has buddhi but no vidya. One can hardly gain favour of the kings with only buddhi and without any vidya. I shall share no part of the wealth that I earn with him. Let him go home.'
>
> The second Brahmin boy agreed with the eldest, and said to the one without learning, 'O! Subuddhi, the one with the discriminating intellect, you should better go home, since you have no vidya, no learning.'

At this, the third Brahmana boy said, 'This is not right. We have played together since early childhood. Our fourth friend should accompany us, and receive an equal share in whatever we earn'.

Because it is said that that wealth is not worth acquiring, which, like the daughter-in-law of a family, is limited to a single person and is not available for the enjoyment of all.

It is also said that the small-minded alone keep calculating who belongs amongst them and who is an outsider. For the large hearted the whole world indeed forms their family: *ayam nijah paro veti gananalaghuchetasam, udaracharitanan tu vasudhaiva kutumbakam.*

'Therefore, let the fourth one amongst us also come along.'

Thus the four of them continued their journey. On the way, in a deep forest, they chanced upon some bones. Seeing these, one of them said, 'Let us put the learning we have acquired to a test. Here are the bones of some dead creature. Let us bring it back to life by the power of our vidya. I shall begin by putting these bones together.'

Saying thus the first Brahmin boy assembled the bones with great enthusiasm, the second provided the skeleton with flesh and blood and covered it with skin, and the third began to infuse life into it.

Before the creature could be brought to life, Subuddhi, the one with the discriminating intellect but without learning, stopped the third one, saying, 'Please wait. What you are creating is a lion. If you give it life, it shall kill us all.'

On being thus obstructed in the practice of his vidya, the third Brahmin boy, retorted, 'Shame upon you! You fool! I shall not let my vidya, my learning, go waste?'

At this Subuddhi said, 'Then please wait a moment, while I climb a tree.'

As Subuddhi climbed up the tree, the third scholar breathed life into the lion. And the lion immediately killed all the three. Later, Subuddhi climbed down the tree and went home.

That is why it is said that buddhi, the discriminating intellect, is better than vidya, mere technical learning. The learned devoid of the discriminating intellect are destroyed, like the Brahmanas who brought the dead lion to life: *varam buddhir na sa vidya vidyaya buddhir uttama, buddhihina vinasyanti yatha te singhakarkah.*

Mahatma Gandhi's rejection of machinery and technology was in continuation with such traditions of dependence of buddhi, which formed scepticism and ambivalence about technological contraptions and technical knowledge. In India this scepticism and ambivalence is rooted on the fundamentals of *sanatana dharma* that the world is a manifestation of Brahman, the creator Himself; and as such it is certainly beyond human comprehension or manipulation. Because, the world is a manifestation of the divine, it has its own natural ways, and its own inborn discipline and harmony. It is the duty of man to try and learn of the ways of the world so as to ensure that his actions do not violate this inherent discipline, the *dharma* of the world. But it is hardly given to him to comprehend the *dharma* of the world in its entirety or to presume to change the world to serve his ends. Technological contraptions and technical knowledge smack of just such presumptuousness about knowing the ways of the world and putting the world to the service of men; hence the scepticism and ambivalence about such knowledge is natural for a right thinking man.

This conception of the world as a natural entity infused with the divine and thus having its own autonomous and sacrosanct ways of engagement. This conception of the world has been perhaps most fully worked out doctrine in the Indian tradition. The Indians have a special term to describe this, rita, meaning the inborn balance and harmony of the world, for defining the autonomous ways. But the Chinese probably have a similar understanding of the world in their concept of li.[42] We know less about other great civilisations of the world, but it seems that similar conception of natural harmony and balance beyond the reach of men prevailed in all civilisations other than the modern Western civilization.

Scepticism and ambivalence about technological contraptions and technical knowledge did not mean that these traditional civilisations were devoid of any sort of technical knowledge. On the other hand, India and China are known to be the most advanced civilisations of the world, in all aspects including science and technology, until the modern times. These two civilisations had, much before the onset of modernity in the west, accumulated an enormous body of knowledge about, for example, about health and disease; generated voluminous information about the therapeutic properties of materials and their classification; and comprehended diverse phenomena of nature from the perspective of health and disease. They had intensively made studies on the of the space and evolved rigorous mathematical techniques for comprehending the motion of moving bodies in space, and learned to reckon epoch and time on earth on the basis of such motion. They had rigorously studied the phenomena of language and the problems associated with systematic communication and interpretation. They had evolved highly competent techniques of irrigation. They had studied soils and plants, and learned to practice the most efficient agricultural techniques. They had explored the mineral wealth of the earth, and evolved sophisticated techniques of metallurgy and metalworking. They had also studied and developed to a high level the technologies of spinning, weaving and dyeing; of construction; of manufacturing various kinds of materials; and of numerous other activities that man carries out to live well in the world. Other spatially and temporally less extensive and lesser-known civilisations must have also developed and applied similarly high levels of scientific and technological knowledge: though we happen to know less about them.

However, the sciences and technologies ,these civilizations, practised were qualitatively different from the science and technology of the modern West. Specifically Science in these civilisations was carried out not with the urge to control and alter nature, but with the intention to learn of the ways of nature so as to ensure that human actions do not violate her essential balance and harmony of the nature. The scepticism and ambivalence that we have discussed above informed their practise of science and technology at a fundamental level. Their sciences had an attitude of humility. They believed that truth always resided in the world in all its complexity, and their theories were mere devices to help man to comprehend the world to the order his life such as not to violate its inherent truth. Their technological interventions were marked by a strong sense of restraint. They were intended to make man follow the ways of nature, not to transcend it.[43]

Science and technology that has arisen in the modern Western civilisation is the product of an attitude that looks upon nature as an adversary, whose secrets man must unravel in order to control and conquer it. This attitude of carrying out an adversarial questioning of nature has indeed led to spectacular results, especially during the last one hundred years or so. Men's ability to intervene in the phenomena of nature and to put nature at his service has advanced enormously. But, this scientific and technological capability has also given rise to an urgent fear of human intervention causing irrevocable disruption of the balance and harmony of various aspects of nature and irreversible erosion of natural capabilities to sustain and support the socially and biologically diverse forms of life on earth. There is now in the world a deep sense of concern about the sustainability of the human enterprise based on modern science and technology.

To address such concerns meaningfully, man shall have to recover the scepticism and ambivalence about technological contraptions and technical knowledge that formed part of the traditions of civilisations other than the modern West civilization, which Mahatma Gandhi tried hard to revive in India.. Men shall have to learn once again to approach the world with a sense of respect for its inborn autonomous ways (dharma). And he shall have , once again, acquire the humility in his theories and restraint in his practice that comes naturally from such respectful attitude towards the world.

Mahatma Gandhi's life and thought can be of immense help in helping man recover respect for reviving the sanctity of the world. We need to develop humility towards human knowledge and restraint in human action. And the need for recovering such respect, humility and restraint is certainly more urgent today than it was during Mahatma Gandhi's times.

We have discussed several aspects of Mahatma Gandhi's thought and action, and indicated how these remain relevant in the modern times. All these aspects of his thought, as we have tried to emphasise, arise from the anchorage and dependence Mahatma Gandhi had in *sanatana dharma.* In *sanatana dharma*, India has been taught the truth about Brahman's creation and the way of living properly in this world that is not only imbued with divinity but is in fact a manifestation of the divine (Brahman). Mahatma Gandhi arrived in India at a time when India had lost faith in this fundamental truth of her heritage and forgotten herself. He restored the faith of India in *sanatana dharma* and brought her back to the right path. And India, under the leadership of Mahatma Gandhi, not only recovered hope for herself, but also she became a source of hope for the rest of the world. After Mahatma Gandhi, India has once again strayed from this path. It is primarily for India and Indians now to be true to the teachings of the Mahatma, to recover their faith and return to the path of *sanatana dharma.* By being thus true to herself, India shall also be true to the world and fulfill her destined role. This is the lesson that Mahatma Gandhi has taught India. And his lesson remains perpetually relevant.

Notes

1 See Gandhi 1915-1948, A Detailed Chronology, compiled by C. D. Dalal, New Delhi: Gandhi Peace Foundation, 1971. See, also, The Collected Works of Mahatma Gandhi, Vol. 13, New Delhi: The Publications Division, Government of India, 1964. These have been published in a hundred volumes, the first of which appeared in 1958 and the last in 1994.

2 See Dharampal, Bharatiya Chitta Manas and Kala, tr. by J. K. Bajaj, Madras: Centre for Policy Studies, 1993, p. 14.

3 Gandhi 1915-1948, A Detailed Chronology, cited above.

4 Professor Swaminathan in the Santhanam Memorial Lecture delivered at Madras on August 23, 1984 attributed this insight to Ramana Maharshi, who had once commented: "They say that Hanuman is chiranjeevi (immortal). It does not mean that a certain monkey goes on living for ever and ever. It means that there will always be on earth someone who serves Rama as your Gandhi does now."

5 Bhavan's Journal, Vol XXI, No.16, March 2, 1975, pp. 45-48.

6 The Collected Works of Mahatma Gandhi, cited above, Vol. 4, p. 408.

7 The Collected Works of Mahatma Gandhi, cited above, Vol. 21, p. 181.

8 The Collected Works of Mahatma Gandhi, cited above, Vol. 21, p. 246.

9 For a more detailed discussion of the Indian conception of the state and society, see J. Bajaj, "Society Has Its Reasons Too," in J. Bajaj (ed.), Ayodhya and the Future India, Madras: Centre for Policy Studies, 1993; especially pp. 15-20. Also see S. Gurumurthy, "The Inclusive and the Exclusive," in the same book, pp. 150-180. For a revealing analysis of the "natural law" as it prevailed in the classical Chinese society as against the "positive human law" of the West, see Joseph Needham, Science and Civilisation in China, Vol. 2, Cambridge: Cambridge University Press, pp. 518-583.

10 M. K. Gandhi, "Hind *Swaraj*," in The Collected Works of Mahatma Gandhi, cited above, Vol. 10, pp. 6-68.

11 The Collected Works of Mahatma Gandhi, cited above, Vol. 85, pp. 32-33.

12 Discussion below about the eighteenth century polity of Chengalpattu is based on work in progress at the Centre for Policy Studies, Madras. Summary records of the survey in English are available in the Tamilnadu State Archives at Madras, and the original accounts in Tamil are lodged in the Department of Palmle of Manuscripts, Tamil University, Thanjavur. A preliminary compilation and analysis of the data may be seen in J. K. Bajaj and M. D. Srinivas, "Indian Economy and Polity in the Eighteenth Century, The Chengalpattu Survey: 1767-74" in Indian Economy and Polity, Madras: Centre for Policy Studies, 1995, pp. 63-84.

13 The Collected Works of Mahatma Gandhi, cited above, Vol. 10, pp. 49, 51.

14 Mahabharata, Anushasana Parva, 61.32-33. The translation here is from J. K. Bajaj and M. D. Srinivas, Annam Bahu Kurvita: Recollecting the Indian Discipline of Growing and Sharing Food in Plenty, Madras: Centre for Policy Studies, 1996, p. 130. See the chapter "Provider of the Unprovided," pp. 106-130, for a detailed exposition of the classical Indian position on the role and place of the king.

15 James Mill, Evidence to the House of Commons Committee, House of Commons Papers, 1831-32, Vol. XIV, pp. 6-7.

16 See Dharampal, Civil Disobedience and Indian Tradition, Varanasi: Sarva Seva Sangh Prakashan, 1971. Also see Richard Heitler, The Varanasi House Tax Hartal of 1810-11, Indian Economic and Social History Review, 1971, pp. 239-257. The former reproduces original documents concerning the events in Varanasi and other towns.

17 Quoted from Dharapal, 1971, cited above, p. 6.

18 Quoted from Richard Heitler, 1971, cited above, pp. 249-250. This petition is not found in the collection of original documents found in Dharampal, 1971, cited above, though some extracts from the petition are quoted in the Introduction, see p. XXXII.

19 Quoted from Richard Heitler, 1971, cited above, p. 253.

20 Quoted from Dharapal, 1971, cited above, p. 37.

21 The testimony of Erskine in Selections of Papers from the Records of the East India House Relative to the Revenue, Police, Civil and Criminal Justice, Under the Company's Government of India, Vol. II, p. 89. Quoted from Heitler, 1971, cited above, p. 246.

22 The Collected Works of Mahatma Gandhi, cited above, Vol. 87, p. 230.

23 The Collected Works of Mahatma Gandhi, cited above, Vol. 62, p. 468.

24 Srimad Valmikiya Ramayana, Balakanda, I.90.

25 Mahabharata, Santi Parva, 86.24.

26 Mahabharata, Santi Parva, 91.38.

27 Padma Purana, 1.37.88.

28 The Collected Works of Mahatma Gandhi, cited above, Vol. 45, p. 328 (Emphasis added).

29 See Dharampal, Some Aspects of Earlier Indian Society and Polity and Their Relevance to the Present, Pune: New Quest, n.d., pp. 28-29. See also J. K. Bajaj and M. D. Srinivas, Annam Bahu Kurvita, cited earlier, pp. 181-185 and p. 195.

30 For a detailed exegesis of Indian classical literature on the imperative of sharing and caring for others, see J. K. Bajaj and M. D. Srinivas, Annam Bahu Kurvita, Madras, 1996, cited above. The Sanskrit verses and their translations in this section follow the rendering there.]

31 The Collected Works of Mahatma Gandhi, cited above, Vol. 34, p. 458.

32 The Sage of Kanchi, Madras, 1991, pp. 143-44.

33 Apastamba Dharmasutra, 2.25.11.

34 The Collected Works of Mahatma Gandhi, cited above, Vol. 21, p. 248.

35 Mahabharata, Vana Parva, 83-84.

36 The Collected Works of Mahatma Gandhi, cited above, Vol. 10, p. 57-58.

37 The Collected Works of Mahatma Gandhi, cited above, Vol. 10, pp. 26-27.

38 The Collected Works of Mahatma Gandhi, cited above, Vol. 10, pp. 37-38.

39 Quoted from Joseph Needham, Science and Civilisation in China, Vol. 2, Cambridge: Cambridge University Press, p. 124.

40 Yukio Mishima, Spring Snow, translated from the Japanese by Michael Gallagher, New York: Pocket Books, 1973, pp. 27-28.

41 Panchatantra, edited with Hindi translation by Sudhakar Malaviya, Varanasi: Chowkhamba, 1993, pp. 734-737. English translation by the author.

42 For an exposition of the concept of li, see Joseph Needham, Science and Civilisation in China, Vol. 2, Cambridge: Cambridge University Press, chapter 18, especially, pp. 557-562.

43 For a somewhat more detailed analysis of these issue, see J. K. Bajaj, "Francis Bacon, the First Philosopher of Modern Science: A Non-Western View" in Ashis Nandy (ed.), Science, Hegemony and Violence: A Requiem for Modernity, Tokyo: United Nations University, 1988, reprint, Oxford India Paperback, 1990, pp. 24-67.

Footnotes

Prahrishtamudito lokas tushtah pushtah sudharmaikahniramayo hy arogas ca durbhikshabhayavarjitah[24]

Contributors

Rewati Raman Pandey (Late), Vice Chancellor of Gorakhpur University

Siddheshwar R. Bhatt, Ex-Professor, University of Delhi, Delhi, India

Musashi Tachikawa, Professor, Faculty of Letters, Aichigakuin University, Nagoya, Japan and Professor Emeritus, the National Museum of Ethnology, Osaka, Japan

Masahiro Shimoda, Professor, Department of Indian Philosophy and Buddhist Studies, Graduate School of Humanities and Sociology, The University of Tokyo

Shinji Shigematsu, Professor, Faculty of Asian Cultural Studies, Outemon Gakuin University, Osaka, Japan

Sudha Malaiya, Director, Ojaswini Institute, Bhopal, India

Prof. N. Vijaya, Department of Sociology, Osmania University, Hyderabad, India

J. K. Bajaj, Center for Policy Studies, Chennai, India

Sengaku Mayeda, President, The Eastern Institute, Japan